Bill and Pam have given parents the guidebook they've been looking for. With refreshing honesty born out of experience, the Farrels share both wisdom and practical strategy for talking with your kids about sex. If you are a parent, you need this book.

—**Jill Savage,** mother of five, founder and CEO of Hearts at Home

◆ ◆ ◆ ◆

All studies show that the more positive, healthy sex education they receive from home, the less promiscuous your kids will be. Bill and Pam Farrel have created a great resource to help you with some of the most important questions of your kids' lives. The Farrels will help you have meaningful conversations with your children about one of God's most wonderful gifts—sexuality.

—**Jim Burns PhD,** President of HomeWord Ministries and author of *Teaching Your Children Healthy Sexuality* and *The Purity Code*

◆ ◆ ◆ ◆

Bill and Pam Farrel powerfully impact parents with the need to fight proactively for this next generation. They equip and encourage you to impart truth, vision, and purpose to your children. While encouraging you to commit your children into God's hands, the Farrels will guide you to stand strong during these turbulent times.

—**Julie Hiramine,** founder of Generations of Virtue and author of *Guardians of Purity*

10 Questions Kids Ask About Sex

Bill & Pam Farrel

HARVEST HOUSE PUBLISHERS
EUGENE, OREGON

Unless otherwise indicated, all Scripture quotations are from the Holy Bible, New International Version®, NIV®. Copyright © 1973, 1978, 1984, 2011, by Biblica, Inc.™ Used by permission of Zondervan. All rights reserved worldwide. www.zondervan.com

Verses marked NASB are taken from the New American Standard Bible®, © 1960, 1962, 1963, 1968, 1971, 1972, 1973, 1975, 1977, 1995 by The Lockman Foundation. Used by permission. (www.Lockman.org)

Verses marked MSG are taken from The Message. Copyright © by Eugene H. Peterson 1993, 1994, 1995, 1996, 2000, 2001, 2002. Used by permission of NavPress Publishing Group.

Verses marked KJV are taken from the King James Version of the Bible.

Cover by Left Coast Design, Portland, Oregon

Bill and Pam Farrel are represented by the literary agency of Alive Communications, Inc., 7680 Goddard Street, Ste #200, Colorado Springs, CO 80920.

Cover photos © iStockphoto / svetikd; Yari Arcurs / Shutterstock

10 QUESTIONS KIDS ASK ABOUT SEX
Copyright © 2013 by Bill and Pam Farrel
Published by Harvest House Publishers
Eugene, Oregon 97402
www.harvesthousepublishers.com

ISBN 978-0-7369-4919-4 (pbk.)
ISBN 978-0-7369-4920-0 (eBook)

Printed in the United States of America

13 14 15 16 17 18 19 20 21 / BP-CD / 10 9 8 7 6 5 4 3 2 1

To all those who were in our youth groups, our church,
our Fellowship of Christian Athletes huddles—stand strong!

To all of our children and grandchildren—
be lights of righteousness!

To Penny Harrington and Robin Collier, our "Aaron and Hur"—
thanks for holding us up in this battle to rescue a generation!

To Jill Savage of Hearts at Home, our editor, Kathleen, and the courageous
team at Harvest House Publishers—thank you for being brave watchmen
standing guard to protect the hearts, minds, and very lives of children, teens,
and young adults.

To the parents who will read and use this book—
thanks for being a hero to your kids and parents of valor in our society.
The world is a better place because you care.

Be on your guard; stand firm in the faith;
be courageous; be strong. Do everything in love.
1 CORINTHIANS 16:13-14

You whom I love and long for, my joy and crown,
stand firm in the Lord in this way, dear friends!
PHILIPPIANS 4:1

Contents

1

How Can I Talk to You?

Do everything in love.

1 Corinthians 16:14

At some point, every parent and child will ask, "How can I talk to you about this?" The simplest question about sex from the mouth of your child can send shivers up the back of all of us. And our kids will have hundreds of questions about love, sex, dating, and relationships as they grow up! When it does happen, when they do ask those sometimes hard-to-answer questions, we grown-ups often vacillate between feeling all flustered and tongue-tied or traveling clear to the other end of the spectrum and getting a heart-pounding sense of duty to communicate everything on this delicate subject perfectly so as not to warp our children forever. Often we feel much like the parent in this story:

> One day a grade-schooler came home and in the middle of doing her spelling homework she asked her mother, "How do you get babies?"
>
> Flustered, the mother rambled, explaining about the birds and bees and body parts. She waxed on about moral responsibility and wise choices. Her daughter sat wide-eyed and mouth gaping open as she tried to process the barrage of information.

The next day while the little girl sat doing her homework again, she proclaimed to her mother, "Mom! I know
how to make babies!"

Mom smiled, thinking the talk had gone better than
she first thought. Then her daughter said, "Our teacher
told us today. You drop the *y* and add *ies*!

Imperfect in delivery—but this mom's heart was in the right place
because she cared! And you care too. You picked up this book because
you care. You care about your child's, your tween's, or your teen's well-
being. You care about his or her choices. You care about every part of
their lives, even one of the most sensitive, yet most vital areas of their
soul: their sexual identity, sexual choices, and future sexual enjoyment.
You are to be commended. As a parent, you are a cut above average.
You are willing to step out and step into the whirlwind of controversy,
questions, and continual avalanche of information (some good and
some bad) on this topic. You are reaching out and walking into this
unknown place because deep in your heart, you want to protect your
child from pain and provide him or her with the happiest possible
future. If we could give you a medal for being a brave, concerned,
involved parent, we would. You are our hero, but more importantly,
you are a hero to your son or daughter.

What Is a Hero?

Because this book was written during wartime, with the media
daily flashing stories of the heroic, we want to draw a comparison
between you, the parent, and our brave men and women in uniform
who fight to defend our democracy and liberty. They put themselves
in harm's way on our behalf. These heroes do so because they believe
in a greater cause: freedom.

We had the awesome honor of being asked to speak at Walter Reed
Army Medical Center for the soldiers in the Wounded Warrior unit
at a couples' date night. One of the soldiers there shared a list of his
injuries with us: brain trauma, shrapnel throughout his body from an
exploding IED, a broken shoulder, and a leg shattered from the knee

down. The broken leg wasn't discovered for months after the explosion because this soldier just kept using it!

I (Pam) was so overcome with emotion, I fumbled for words. "Oh, dear! That is quite a list! I am thankful you are here…thankful you are alive!"

He replied, "I promised my family I would come home. They can try to blow me up. They can shoot my legs out from under me. They can break my shoulder so bad that with every step it sends excruciating pain throughout my body. But if I can move, if I can crawl, if I can drag myself forward, if my heart is still beating in my body, I will come home—whatever it takes—whatever it takes!"

Everyone within earshot—especially his wife—was crying at his heroism. The soldier had hobbled and crawled for miles, every move sending searing pain through his body. He had vowed to make it to safety so his kids and family could be safer too. His desire to stay alive for his children imprinted a heroic picture of love in my mind. But his words "Whatever it takes, whatever it takes," compelled and motivated us once again to never give up, never give in when it comes to our own children.

Whatever It Takes

The Bible shares a story of a great hero, a hero to our hearts, souls, minds, bodies, and futures. One of the writers of the New Testament, Paul, explained the hero's actions this way:

> In your relationships with one another, have the same mindset as Christ Jesus: Who, being in very nature God, did not consider equality with God something to be used to his own advantage; rather, he made himself nothing by taking the very nature of a servant, being made in human likeness. And being found in appearance as a man, he humbled himself by becoming obedient to death—even death on a cross! Therefore God exalted him to the highest place and gave him the name that is above every name (Philippians 2:5-9).

The hero I'm talking about? Jesus. He wasn't thinking about Himself when He died on the cross. He was thinking about you; He was thinking about me; He was thinking about our kids and His desire to set us all free from the chains of our own sins. We were on His heart and He was so other-centered He did whatever it took to keep us free.

This passage also calls us to follow His other-centered mindset. And this command is repeated numerous times, as in Ephesians 5:1-2: "Follow God's example, therefore, as dearly loved children and walk in the way of love, just as Christ loved us and gave himself up for us." We are to walk in the "way of love"—His sacrificial love. Living with others in mind is heroic because it is counterintuitive. We are all born selfish, after all. Heroism goes against our fallen nature. By nature we would rather opt for self-protection. And that self-protective attitude can make us timid rather than heroic. If you're honest with yourself, when it comes to talking to your children and planning how to best care for and guard their futures, thoughts like these might have already gone through your mind. They've sure gone through ours!

- All this sex talk makes me feel uncomfortable!
- What if I give them stupid advice?
- What if I am not the cool parent anymore?
- What if my child doesn't like what I say?
- What if my child doesn't like me because of my views?
- What if I look bad because I didn't do everything right?

All those statements have the word *me* or *I* in them. They are self-focused. When it comes to helping your child, you have to decide in your heart that it is not about you: It's about your kid and it's about God. When you make that choice, you, as a concerned parent, are placing the needs of your child first. That is a heroic decision.

Heroes Need Help Too

Heroes don't have to know everything. Here are some legitimate questions you might ask yourself as you teach your child about sex:

- How do I know when to begin talking about sex with my child?

- What do I say? When should I say it? And where should it be said?

- How can I balance protecting my child's innocence yet make him or her savvy enough to not follow the crowd or be abused?

- Who can I trust to help me figure this out?

- What do I do if I made mistakes in the area of sex and dating? How can I give advice to my own kid when I messed up so badly?

- How can I be tactful and tasteful yet specific and accurate?

- How can I handle my own pain or fears if I was abused, yet still hand down a positive view of sex to my kids?

- Where do I find the guts to do this?

You are not alone in your questions, fears, or discomfort. One journal in pediatric medicine explains,

> Because most parents do not feel comfortable or competent talking with their adolescents about sexual issues, they tend to limit conversations to "safe" topics, such as developmental changes (e.g., menstruation and other pubertal changes), impersonal aspects of sexuality (e.g., reproductive facts), and negative consequences, such as AIDS and sexually transmitted diseases. In contrast, parents tend to avoid or cover in a cursory way more private topics, such as masturbation, the psychological and experiential aspects of sexuality such as orgasm or sexual decision-making, and how to obtain and use condoms. It is, therefore, not surprising that a significant majority of both adolescents and parents feel dissatisfied with such restricted communication about sexuality. In general, teenagers perceive a gap between the topics that their parents cover during sexual

discussions and the more delicate topics about which they are concerned.[1]

It is our goal in this book to lessen your stress—and the stress on your children—by offering some easy-to-use researched information, quick-to-find tools, and helpful conversation starters. And we'll try to make you laugh along the way, because there's nothing like laughter to take the awkwardness out of having "the talk!"

A Battle for Love

Why spend so much time reminding you that you're the hero of your kids' hearts and lives? Because it's a battle out there! What with the discourse and dialogue about sexual choices, the definition of marriage and family, the discussion of what is right, moral, pure, good, and healthy, the most intimate, personal issue of all—sex—can become a battlefield strewn with land mines.

There are two opposing ways to view sex: One is God's, the other, Satan's. God's view is that sexual love is made for what *I can give*. It is to be protected through the context of marriage. Satan tells us that sex is for what *I can get*. In this view, sex is to be exploited until it uses up everyone in its path.

On September 11, 2001, thousands of men, women, and children died at the hands of terrorists. The terrorists succeeded in their destruction in part because America was taken by surprise. Who would ever think of such a heinous crime as to fly planes full of innocent people into an office building full of *more* innocent people? Only those who embody evil could hatch that plot. We wrote this book so you will not be taken by surprise as a parent. Be assured, the evil one is hatching plenty of plots to ravage the children we love so dearly.

The enemy of our soul wants to "steal and kill and destroy" while Jesus says He came that we "may have life, and have it to the full" (John 10:10). God also gave us all the ingredients to make relationships function in a healthy manner: The fruit of the Spirit is "love, joy, peace, forbearance, kindness, goodness, faithfulness, gentleness and self-control." And God's definition of love is clear:

> Love is patient, love is kind. It does not envy, it does not boast, it is not proud. It does not dishonor others, it is not self-seeking, it is not easily angered, it keeps no record of wrongs. Love does not delight in evil but rejoices with the truth. It always protects, always trusts, always hopes, always perseveres. Love never fails (1 Corinthians 13:4-8).

And that is what we all want for our kids, right? We want them to be able to produce an enduring love that protects, perseveres, and provides a life filled with love, joy, peace, patience, kindness, goodness, faithfulness, gentleness, and fidelity. And if you are like us, you pray that someday each of your children will find someone to love them this same wonderful way.

Teaming up with God to help your children reach the goal of loving by God's design and being loved that way in return will take your heroic love. Your parental love must become a love that always perseveres and a love that does whatever it takes to provide the best for your son's or daughter's future.

Statistically speaking, most of the people who read this book will have some chapters they wish they could forget in their past. They wish they had done a few things differently growing up. But it's time to set aside shame, guilt, and finger-pointing. Some of you didn't know God's plan for love, so how could you follow it? Others had a rebellious, wild-oats-sowing season of your life and you might have regrets. We don't want you to feel any worse than you probably already do. We just want to help you help your own kids. That's what heroic love does. It sets aside self-interest for the greater good of another.

Commit now to set aside your own issues and do what's best for your kids. Are you willing to be heroic, no matter how much time, talent, energy, bravery, and resources it takes?

A Sacred Wedding Is Heroic

Two of our three children are married now, and we are delighted with their choices of a life partner. We prayed for those dear daughters-in-law for many years! And like us, you might already be praying for the person God has in mind for each of your children. We prayed specifically and daily for the young ladies each of our sons would someday marry. I (Pam) remember praying this prayer for our child's future spouse the day we got the news we were going to have our first baby. We prayed many things for that baby still in utero:

- that the child would form safely
- that he or she would love God completely
- that he or she would follow God wholeheartedly
- that he or she would be protected from the evil of this world
- that he or she would reach the God-given plan for his or her life
- that he or she would one day take full responsibility and decide to make wise choices
- that he or she would someday find a mate who also loved God with a whole heart

And on each wedding day, as that bride walked down the aisle, all those prayers of all those days echoed in our hearts and minds. That beautiful bride, that handsome groom, joined their lives in holy matrimony. It was a sacred moment. They would form a new family and the values we held so dear would pass from our generation to a generation yet to come. That is exactly God's goal: to pass Christ-centered values and His plan of love from generation to generation:

> One generation commends your works to another;
>   they tell of your mighty acts.
> They speak of the glorious splendor of your majesty—
>   and I will meditate on your wonderful works.
> They tell of the power of your awesome works—
>   and I will proclaim your great deeds.
> They celebrate your abundant goodness
>   and joyfully sing of your righteousness.

The Lord is gracious and compassionate,
slow to anger and rich in love.
Psalm 145:4-8

Wedding days are filled with happiness, joy, and love. The wedding ceremony is the vessel that demonstrates that love to the world. As people observe the love shared between the two people exchanging their vows, they gain the opportunity to see God and His love. The closer the couple is walking with Jesus, the better their love radiates God's love.

We have been trained in all kinds of outreach and evangelistic methods, but it is the simple love we share that has had more people asking us, "What do you have that makes your lives and marriage so different from mine?" At that moment, we have the delightful opportunity of sharing how anyone can receive and be lavished in the love of God. All they need to do is surrender to His plan and His path for their future— plans that God promises will give them "hope and a future" (Jeremiah 29:11).

Sharing a vibrant sexual life in the marriage bed is one of the ways God shares a picture of His love. When it works the way He intended it to, sex in a healthy relationship is a real-life portrait of God's relationship with us. Sex within marriage is one of God's strongest tools of connecting a couple so their love best reflects the unity and passion of His love. Since relationships are at the core of how God communicates His love to us, let's take a look at His view on this gift of sex.

God's Ladder of Love

When you're climbing a ladder, you start out with the first rung and then climb to the next—and then the next rung after that. Follow this progression with us.

Sex Was God's Idea

Sex was God's secret a long time before it was "Victoria's Secret." God initiated the idea of sex to keep the human race going. He could have decided on any technique, but He elected for a relationship; an act of biology so intricate that it worked at its best between two people who were committed to each other for a lifetime. To ensure this model would work, God set up the human race by creating just one man and one woman—two who were literally "a match made in heaven."

> The man gave names to all the livestock, the birds in the sky and all the wild animals. But for Adam no suitable helper was found. So the Lord God caused the man to fall into a deep sleep; and while he was sleeping, he took one of the man's ribs and then closed up the place with flesh. Then the Lord God made a woman from the rib he had taken out of the man, and he brought her to the man. The man said, "This is now bone of my bones and flesh of my flesh; she shall be called 'woman,' for she was taken out of man." That is why a man leaves his father and mother and is united to his wife, and they become one flesh. Adam and his wife were both naked, and they felt no shame (Genesis 2:20-25).

What a great picture of sex in a committed relationship! You could say God performed the first wedding ceremony when he actually *created* Eve for Adam! God ordained a one-man, one-woman marriage from the very beginning. In that context, this couple could be naked and not feel any shame. There were no others at the creation of marriage—just this one man and one woman. From their union the whole history of humankind would be produced.

Marriage Was God's Idea

The first place we see God endorsing sex in this new marriage in the garden is at the Creation:

> So God created mankind in his own image, in the image of God he created them; male and female he created them. God blessed them and said to them, "Be fruitful and increase in number; fill the earth and subdue it" (Genesis 1:27-28).

Sex in marriage was created before the fall of mankind. Can you imagine sex with the perfect person God created for you, in an unadulterated environment, natural and wholesome, with no negatives attached because Satan hadn't yet entered the scene? (It was *after* Satan tempted Eve that things like PMS and pain in childbirth were set in place.) Sex before the fall had no shame, no guilt, no pain…it was all good!

Marriage Is a Reflection of Christ's Relationship with the Church

> "For this reason a man will leave his father and mother and be united to his wife, and the two will become one flesh." This is a profound mystery—but I am talking about Christ and the church (Ephesians 5:31-32).

Did you catch that last bit? God designed sex to be a reflection of Christ's love and Christ's commitment to the church. Inversely, it would seem, sex outside the bounds of matrimony, sex not carried out according to those biblical passages, is *not* a reflection of Christ's relationship toward us. That is exactly what Satan wants—sex that's distorted and all about what it can get! Satan wants to rob from your child's future instead of preserving one of the most special gifts God ever designed for him or her.

Sex in Marriage Was God's Idea

That is exactly why Satan *hates* the entire notion of love, marriage, and the pure, holy use of sex within the context of marriage. It gives God glory, and the devil hates that! Satan wants the glory all to himself, and that is why he is literally hell-bent on distorting sexuality, twisting love, and mocking the value of integrity, fidelity, holiness, and obedience to Jesus. And Satan will do anything to win, even if it is destroying the love life, physical wellness, or future of your child.

Which leads us back to why you are so heroic, Mom and Dad. You are standing in the way of Satan's plan for ruining your child's life and future. You are the precious protector and guardian of his or her destiny.

Your goal is to protect your child while you equip him or her to protect their own life with good choices and decisions.

You Hold the Keys

Mom and Dad, you hold the key to your child's future. Our friend Dave told us a beautiful story about this that penetrated me to the core. When his daughter Jody was a very little girl, she came home and announced her love interest in a little boy. Dave said to her, "Honey, when you are much older, there will be a day when you will want to give your heart to a man. He will have to be really special, and you will need to feel confident that he is the one God wants you to marry. Until then, I will keep your heart. I will keep it safe."

Dave's wife made a heart that hung in their home. On it hung two gold keys, one for each daughter. Anytime Dave prayed with his daughters, tucked them into bed, or performed any of the other daily interactions a loving father would have with his daughter, he'd say, "And who has the key to your heart?" His daughters would answer, "You do, Daddy." Anytime he had to set a rule or make a correction he would begin with, "Remember who has the key to your heart?" And the girls would answer, "You do, Daddy." Then Dave would explain that because he, their daddy, had their best interests on his heart, he had to make decisions and choices to protect and provide the very best path for his daughters. Dave would explain, "God has called me to do this because God and Daddy love both of you little girls very much."

Dave shared, "One day Jody met and fell in love with a fabulous man, Chris. She came to me and asked if she could have her heart now because she had found the man she wanted to give it to. I agreed and prayed and released her heart."

On the day of their wedding, Dave asked Jody one last time, "Who has the key to your heart?" But this time the answer was different. It was the name of her new husband.[2]

You, Mom and Dad, hold the key to both protect your child now and provide a hope for a happy future in his or her marriage. It is as if you are a security guard for an invaluable treasure.

Emergency Broadcast—This Is Not a Test!

We're all aware of the emergency warning systems alerting us to things like flash floods, hurricanes, and tornadoes. I wish that same sound would go off when adults shirked their calling—I know I would like that kind of obvious signal!

In the area of sexuality, moral integrity, and fighting for the purity and futures of our children, we are in a state of emergency. This is not a test! Consider just a few of the more startling statistics:

- Nearly half of U.S. high school students surveyed in 2011 had had sex, a third of them in the previous three months. Of these, almost 40 percent did not use a condom and 77 percent did not use birth control. About 15 percent of these students had had sex with four or more partners.[3]

- Eighty percent of *evangelical* young adults (ages 18 to 29) say they have had sex before marriage. Of these, 64 percent have done so within the last year and 42 percent are in a current sexual relationship.[4]

- In 2009, more than half of births to American women under 30 occurred outside marriage.[5]

- Worldwide there are approximately 42 million abortions every year.[6] In 2008 there were 1.21 million in the United States alone—that's 3,321 abortions every day.[7]

- One woman in four will be sexually assaulted during her lifetime. In a survey, one in twelve college men admitted to raping women. Thirty-five percent of college men indicated that they would rape a woman if they could be assured of not getting caught.[8] (Getting caught is helping: DNA evidence has lowered the incidence of rape in the United States.)

- Adolescents and young adults are at the greatest risk for acquiring an STD such as AIDS, chlamydia, gonorrhea, syphilis, and genital herpes. About 19 million new infections occur each year, almost half of them among people aged 15 to 24.[9]

- 50,000 new HIV infections occur each year in the United States. In 2009, young persons accounted for 39 percent of all new HIV infections in the US.[10] There is still no known cure for the death sentence of HIV/AIDS. Medicines only lengthen life and lessen symptoms.

Add to this all the gender identity confusion fueled by homosexual activists like Daniel Villarreal, who admits that gay activists actually do want to indoctrinate America's children: "We want educators to teach future generations of children to accept queer sexuality," he says. "In fact, our very future depends on it." He bragged that their agenda was even broader than mere indoctrination. "I and a lot of other people want to indoctrinate, recruit, teach, and expose children to queer sexuality *and there is nothing wrong with that*" [emphasis his]. Writing in response to opposition of the same-sex marriage bill in New York, Villarreal said, "Recruiting children? You bet we are."[11]

What is the outcome of all this? Rebecca Hagelin, author of *30 Ways in 30 Days to Save Your Family*, notes, "A sea of teenagers are living with regret. 55 percent of the boys and 70 percent of the girls who had sex now say they wish they had not."[12]

Mom and Dad, they need your help to rescue them from becoming a statistic.

Respond to the Emergency

Obviously God wants us to respond to what is going on around our children and in this culture. But what are we to do? First, be a watchman. In Ezekiel 3:17 God rouses the prophet: "Son of man, I have made you a watchman for the people of Israel; so hear the word I speak and give them warning from me." You are like the sentry or watchman making rounds or stationed on a wall as a lookout—and your task is to be vigilant. But vigilant doing what? What's a watchman supposed to do?

Watchmen work around the clock. "I have posted watchmen on your walls, Jerusalem; they will never be silent day or night" (Isaiah 62:6).

Watchmen patrol the streets to preserve order. "The watchmen found me as they made their rounds in the city" (Song of Songs 3:3).

Watchmen sound a warning. "When the lookout standing on the tower in Jezreel saw Jehu's troops approaching, he called out, 'I see some troops coming'" (2 Kings 9:17).

Watchmen submit their duty to God. "Unless the LORD watches over the city, the guards stand watch in vain" (Psalm 127:1).

Watchmen are vigilant at all times. "Go, post a lookout and have him report what he sees…let him be alert, fully alert" (Isaiah 21:6-7).

In the Old Testament, God shows us how seriously He takes the role of the watchman:

> When I bring the sword against a land, and the people of the land choose one of their men and make him their watchman, and he sees the sword coming against the land and blows the trumpet to warn the people, then if anyone hears the trumpet but does not heed the warning and the sword comes and takes their life, their blood will be on their own head. Since they heard the sound of the trumpet but did not heed the warning, their blood will be on their own head. If they had heeded the warning, they would have saved themselves. But if the watchman sees the sword coming and does not blow the trumpet to warn the people and the sword comes and takes someone's life, that person's life will be taken because of their sin, but I will hold the watchman accountable for their blood. Son of man, I have made you a watchman for the people of Israel; so hear the word I speak and give them warning from me (Ezekiel 33:1-7).

Now God set this principle in place in the Old Testament because in addition to the spiritual battle zone they found themselves in, Israel was waging a physical war for their very survival as a nation. That is not what we are dealing with (at least not yet!), so the consequence for slacking is not death, but the point is clear: The watchman's job was so vital that a stiff penalty was in store for those who shirked on their duty. Today, if you make an error as a parent, God *is not* going to wipe you off the face of the earth.

However, if you miss something important in your son's or daughter's life or surroundings, chances are you will have a bigger battle on your hands. Anytime anyone steps out of God's design for living, things get confusing, messy, and sometimes traumatic. Being a watchman is work, but not watching out will just lead to more work! So being a watchman is a prudent choice for a parent to make.

Our kids need a watchman in us because there are really only two ways to live: smarter or harder. Following God's path is smarter (though you and your child will need to be diligent to learn then walk God's best path). And not following God's plan is definitely harder. It is hard to deal with your child's pain after someone has used him or her for their own sexual gratification. It's hard to manage an unplanned pregnancy. It's hard to watch a heart slowly harden toward a walk with Jesus. All those things are much harder than being vigilant up front. Being a watchman is definitely the smarter way to go.

In the book of Isaiah comes an intriguing question: "Watchman, how far gone is the night? Watchman, how far gone is the night?" (Isaiah 21:11 NASB). We're deeper into the night than we think.

Here's one example from the book *You're Teaching My Child What?*

> I'd been invited to speak at a small private college outside Philadelphia. The auditorium was filled to capacity...After [my talk] I asked for questions, and a number of hands shot up...A dark-haired girl in the front row raised her hand. "I'm a perfect example of what you talked about. I always used condoms, but I got HPV anyway, and it's one of the high-risk types. I had an abnormal Pap test, and next week I'm going to have a colposcopy...But I thought it over," she continued, "and I decided that the pleasure I had with my partners was worth it."[13]

This is a mind that has lost its ability to reason, or has never learned how to reason at all. Either way, it is far into the night. The risk of death was not as important to this young woman as a few moments of sexual pleasure. The author goes on to write, "She'll never know—is the virus gone, or just dormant? Had anyone told her that having one sexually transmitted disease makes her more vulnerable to others, including HIV? That being on the pill could increase her risk, and that pregnancy can re-activate the virus?"[14]

The night is getting darker. People young and old are losing their bearings, their ability to make vital, life-saving decisions. That is why God is looking for heroes—ordinary moms, dads, leaders, teachers, and youth workers who will hold the torch of His original plan for love and intimacy. God is looking for you! Be a watchman, and be able to say, "Day after day, my lord, I stand on the watchtower; every night I stay at my post" (Isaiah 21:8).

If Not You, Then Whom?

If we as parents neglect to instruct, lead, guide, and dialogue with our kids, then where will they get the information to make decisions and form their views? They will be swayed by the media, by friends, and by the educational system.

The Media

American children spend more than 38 hours a week using media. That includes television, videos, music, computers and video games. One study showed that 75 percent of all music videos include sexual images. More than half are also violent—usually against women. The average teen will come across nearly 14,000 sexual references in the media each year. Only about one percent of these will talk about birth control or the risk of pregnancy and STDs.[15]

Dr. Dave Currie of Doing Family Right Ministries shares a story of how even well-meaning parents and grandparents can be forced to clean up the mess media so easily can make:

> A father had approached me with the tragic story of how well-meaning grandparents had given an iPad to a much-loved grandchild. This 11-year-old, with her curiosity and a push from her peers, had googled the word "sex." She was

traumatized. Thankfully, she came to her parents about her extreme confusion to talk and pray through the defiling impact these sexual images had had on her.[16]

Friends

If not the media, what about the influence of friends? Dr. Currie continues his story:

> Don't say it can't happen to your family. It did ours. When my youngest daughter was at a sleepover for a friend's thirteenth birthday party, the girls, in daring and unsupervised group fashion, managed to get on an adults-only dating website. They thought they would have fun creating a fictitious profile but used their pictures. It went from innocent though stupid to dangerous when one girl went back later and put real contact information for our daughter—*our phone number!* I am so glad God protected us as I was the one who received the call from an older man wanting to speak to her. He back-peddled hard when he found out she was just 13 and I was her dad![17]

That is a picture of the mayhem media can cause—but also how valuable it is to have a hero for a dad!

You will hear much more about media, its influence, how to manage it, and how to monitor it in your kids' lives in coming chapters. We'll also discuss the role of good and not-so-good peer choices. Stay tuned!

School

We might think we are safe to delegate sex education to the school—but is that actually the best choice? Dr. Miriam Grossman pulls back the curtain on what schools are really teaching our kids:

> Parents, if you believe that the goals of sexuality education are to prevent pregnancy and disease, you are being hoodwinked. You must understand that these curricula

are rooted in an ideology that you probably don't share. This ideology values, above all—health, science, or parental authority—sexual freedom....

...Do you want instructors, whose personal values might be at odds with yours, to encourage your kids to question what they've been taught at home and at church, and to come up with their own worldview based on taking sexual risks that endanger their health and wellbeing? It seems reasonable to question the ethics of this practice.

What these "experts" are hiding is their goal of bringing about radical social change, one child at a time...From a review of many of today's sex ed curricula and websites, it would appear that a "sexually healthy" individual is one who has been "desensitized," who is without any sense of embarrassment or shame (what some might consider "modesty"), whose sexuality is always "positive" and "open," who respects and accepts "diverse" lifestyles, and who practices "safer sex" with every "partner."

This is not about health, folks. This is about indoctrination.[18]

In coming chapters we will look more intently at sex education, who should do it, and when. We'll look at what parts (if any) you might want to delegate and, if you outsource any pieces, whom do you trust? And what do you say and when to help your son or daughter make wise, godly choices in the future?

Your job as a watchman is to work yourself out of a job. While your children are younger you are the watchman on the wall, but in their tween and teen years you will be giving them on-the-job training to become a watchman over their own lives. As they gain the heartbeat of God, they will take over their own lives, choices, and decisions. They will develop their own inner moral compass. The long-term goal is that you will raise children who will grow so strong, articulate, smart, and capable that they will positively influence the culture around them, and the culture will begin to better reflect the heart of God and His plan for this world.

Can We Talk?

One day your child will ask, "Can we talk?" (At least that is what we hope and pray they will do—ask you!) You'll need to have some basic principles in place to help you best respond to the questions he or she poses. In each chapter, we will give you some helpful sidebars, real illustrations, useful lists, vital statistics, and other "need-to-find-quickly" information. And for those talks with your son or daughter we will provide a checklist of bullet points in the "Answers to Have Ready" section. This way, as you are discussing each particular area you will have the broad brush strokes that you can then personalize and mold into your own words.

We will also provide what we call Parent-to-Parent talking points so you can form valid, sustainable conversation with other moms and dads—some of whom may not always agree with you. In the world we all live in, with a majority of the population lacking a solid internal moral compass based on a biblical worldview, it is vital to prepare yourself well. This way you can, in turn, prepare your children well to defend your beliefs, values, and morals and represent them to the glory of God in the public arena. Often these conversations just appear on the soccer sidelines, as you work on a school project with other parents, over a dinner out, or at a family gathering. You may also be called to represent Christ's worldview on sexuality, gender, or moral choices in the public square, on social media, in the boardroom, or in the classroom. We hope these bullet points and some of the resources we point you to will help you as you prepare your words.

Whether you are debating and dialoging with adults, seeking to explain the birds and bees to a child, or formulating your thoughts for a vital talk with your teen, know that no matter how much you prepare, at some point you can (and need to) relax and trust God. He promises He will be with you:

> You'll end up on the witness stand, called to testify. Make up your mind right now not to worry about it. I'll give you the words and wisdom that will reduce all your accusers to stammers and stutters (Luke 21:13-15 MSG).

If you do whatever I command you and walk in obedience to me and do what is right in my eyes by obeying my decrees and commands, as David my servant did, I will be with you (1 Kings 11:38).

When you pass through the waters, I will be with you; and when you pass through the rivers, they will not sweep over you. When you walk through the fire, you will not be burned; the flames will not set you ablaze. For I am the LORD your God, the Holy One of Israel, your Savior (Isaiah 43:2-3).

Answers to Have Ready

Here are the basic talking points for that first conversation (and all the rest yet to come). More details will be in future chapters, but keep these principles in mind as you prepare to dialogue with your child or teen.

Talk First

Talk about body parts, touching, and the fundamentals of how babies are made. Cover the basic biology before they hear about it on the playground. Talk about body changes before they happen and feelings for the opposite gender before they are interested in the opposite sex. Talk about healthy, God-ordained sex in marriage before you have to deal with distortions of sex by Satan.

Talk Enough

Give them 20 percent more information than they ask for. Be tactfully explicit—not abstract. Answer the question with a short answer first, wait for a response, and then offer more details as you need to.

Talk Positively

Positive messages are better than negative. Instead of saying "don't do this or that," try to reframe it into an affirmative. For example, instead of telling a tween or teen that premarital sex is bad, so don't do it, tell them that sex is a good gift and that is why it is to be protected until expressed in marriage.

Talk Honestly

Use accurate medical terms instead of nicknames for body parts. Be straightforward and tell your child why you want to talk about the next layer of sexual information. And if you lacked in judgment in an area growing up, share this information at an age-appropriate time.

Talk, Then Listen

Learn to listen, not just lecture. Practice questions like: Have you heard the term _____? Do you know what _____ is? What have you heard from friends about _____? How do you feel about what I just shared? Do you have any questions about what I shared with you?

Talk Wisely

Help your child gain a moral compass, good decision-making skills, and the confidence to act on what God whispers to his or her heart. Place sex within the context for which God created it. Get your ducks in a row and be prepared for what you think might be the next sexual question or topic that might come up. If surprised, feel free to say, "Wow, that's a great question. Let me get some information together for you and we'll chat about this later (today, tomorrow, over a burger, etc.)."

Talk Calmly

Don't freak out. Some topics might come up before you want them to. Try to talk with your child gently and reasonably, without getting emotional or frazzled. Take a few breaths, pray, take a walk, or whatever you need to do so that your emotions are in check and stable.

Talk in a Positive Place

If you make the place and experience a positive one each time you discuss sexual matters, your child will connect sex talks to feelings of closeness with you and/or your spouse. He or she might link these moments to happy, joyful, or positive emotions if they take place in a calm location: sitting on your bed or the child's or over ice cream, a burger, or other favorite food. (Our sons preferred all our talks to take place over steak or carne asada burritos!) For those "big talks" we often would link them to a fun family activity, like boating, skiing, a day at the beach, or a family picnic.

Talk after Praying

As you pray for your child, God will give you insights either through His Word or through the leading of His Holy Spirit. He will help you find the words to use and the best time to lead your child to make wiser choices. Don't worry: He'll give you all the specifics to best prepare you for success as you lead your child to make wise choices.

Talk Expecting Your Child Wants to Talk

Your son or daughter wants to hear from you. Here's what one survey tells us:

> More than half of 12th grade girls (53%) said that during their high school years they wanted to be able to talk to their parents about love and relationships. Nearly four in 10 (39%) wanted to be able to talk with their parents about sex...As they look ahead to the years immediately after high school, those numbers remain largely unchanged. Half (50%) still want to talk to their parents about love and relationships...Forty percent say they want to be able to talk about sex with their parents once they're out of high school.[19]

Talk United

It might seem easier to talk to Mom, but the united two-parent approach has the best outcome.[20] In addition, those teens who live in intact homes with Dad involved are much less likely to be involved in premarital sex and risky behaviors.[21] In our work as youth pastors, in the senior pastorate, and as the parents of three sons, we have seen that having the father involved makes a tremendous difference. If Dad is available as a positive, active role model for his sons and daughters, the children will make better choices. It is in your child's best interest (if possible) to involve both parents in discussions on love, sex, and dating.

Bring God into the Talk

Moral and religious convictions do make a difference. One study indicated that girls were less likely to have premarital sex if their mothers cited moral or religious reasons in their discussions. (Conversely, the more liberal the daughter perceived her mother's values to be, the more likely she was to have sex—and have it younger and with more partners.[22]) In a recent study, 45 percent of boys ages 15 to 19 cited religion to be a factor in their sexual decisions.[23]

Talk Because It Makes a Difference

According to authors Stan and Brenna Jones, "The closer the child says his or her relationship is with parents, the less likely the child is to be having sex. A close relationship between parent and child appears to instill in the child the desire to want to live out the values and moral beliefs of the parent."[24] In a national survey more than nine of ten teens agreed that among the benefits of waiting to have sex is enjoying the respect of parents.[25] Mom and Dad—you *do* make a difference!

God is with you. God is with your child. Together you can be a winning team—a heroic team—building a future to look forward to.

Parent to Parent

You will be a better role model for a healthy attitude toward sex if you have a clear view of just why God created sex. We thought we'd share a thumbnail sketch with you of the five reasons God created "Red-Hot Monogamy"—because if we as parents are comfortable and well-centered in our sexuality, it will be easier to have those much-needed discussions with our children and teens.

God Gave Us Sex for Procreation

Be fruitful and increase in number (Genesis 1:22).

The human race is perpetuated through sexual union: One egg is fertilized by one sperm.

God Gave Us Sex for Recreation

> And it came to pass, when he had been there a long time, that Abimelech king of the Philistines looked out at a window, and saw, and, behold, Isaac was sporting with Rebekah his wife (Genesis 26:8 KJV).

Sex within the context of marriage is to be enjoyed.

God Gave Us Sex for Reconnection

> Do not deprive each other except by mutual consent and for a time, so that you may devote yourselves to prayer. Then come together again so that Satan will not tempt you because of your lack of self-control (1 Corinthians 7:5).

Sex is meant to keep couples emotionally, physically, and spiritually connected.

God Gave Us Sex for Rejuvenation

> Strengthen me with raisins, refresh me with apples, for I am faint with love (Song of Solomon 2:5).

Sex within marriage is good for our emotional and physical wellness.

God Gave Us Sex for Proclamation

> He who loves his wife loves himself. After all, no one ever hated their own body, but they feed and care for their body, just as Christ does the church—for we are members of his body. "For this reason a man will leave his father and mother and be united to his wife, and the two will become one flesh." This is a profound mystery—but I am talking about Christ and the church (Ephesians 5:28-32).

Sex is a picture of the complete love and commitment intended for marriage. Marriage reflects Christ's love for the church.

Answers for Your Heart

Before you have answers for your child, you need to ask yourself a few questions and get some answers. You may want to get a journal and answer these or grab a cup of coffee and discuss them with your spouse. You can also use them for a discussion group of moms or co-ed parent study to help prepare for a lifestyle of building a great relationship with your child or teen.

- Looking back, how comfortable are you with your own sexual choices growing up?

- The best thing you can do for your child's future is to provide an intact two-parent family or, if single, an extended family that will partner with you to provide the much-needed role of the absent parent. What can you do to either strengthen your marriage or create an extended family support network?

- How do you feel about talking with your child at the different ages:

  as a toddler/preschooler
  as a grade school student
  as a tween
  as a teen
  as a college student or young adult
  as an adult

- What would best prepare you to feel ready for conversations with your child or teen?

- How can you move forward in getting your own heart, mind, and emotions ready for the parenting God has in front of you?

Do You Love Me?

But those who plan what is good find love and faithfulness.

Proverbs 14:22

Most parents have a goodnight ritual with their children. We loved cuddling and sharing favorite children's books like *Goodnight Moon, Love You Forever,* or *Runaway Bunny.* Many parents borrow lines from these books to express their love, telling their children, "I'll love you forever!" We had a "Who loves you more?" game. Our kids had a stick-on solar system on their ceiling. When the lights went off it glowed in the dark. That glow-in-the-dark solar system helped our game! Our ritual after praying was to switch off the light and give them each a hug, and before we left the room it might sound like this:

Mom: Night-night. I love you!

Preschooler: Love you more.

Mom: I love you to our church.

Preschooler: I love you to Grandma's house.

Mom: I love you to the end of the ocean.

Preschooler: I love you to the top of the mountain.

Mom: I love you to the moon.

Preschooler: I love you to the sun.

Mom: I love you to heaven where Jesus lives.

Preschooler: I love you to infinity!

Mom: You win! But I love you to infinity and back again!

Preschooler: You win too!

The game could never end until someone got to infinity—and back again. Over the years, some of the places we could "love you" to were unusual or exotic—or silly. But it got all our creative juices flowing. This also reinforced some knowledge of geography and science, but more importantly, our kids were convinced that we loved them and we would travel great distances to show them our love!

Do You Love Me Enough?

One of the other occasional tests of your love that is necessary, but not enjoyable, is discipline. In our home, the need for physical discipline was rare. However, for direct rebellion or (especially) to keep a child from danger, for a brief window of time in each of our children's lives, we did use corporal punishment. (This was during those early years of preschool before they had reasoning or verbal skills that come later in preschool or kindergarten.) We detail all the strict guidelines, our basis for how and when we used this parenting tool, and the biblical guidelines for discipline of all modes in our book *The 10 Best Decisions a Parent Can Make*. Here we will share just a short, humorous story to make the point that discipline might not be fun for you—or your child—but it is sometimes very necessary and it has a good purpose if applied biblically.

We were visiting my brother, his wife, and their brand-new baby for Thanksgiving. They lived in a historic ranch house 13 miles down a dirt road and over an hour from the nearest city. Their heat source was a wood-burning stove. The stove sat on a brick hearth that was raised about three inches off the floor. It was easy to forget it was there and trip if you weren't paying attention. We brought our two-year-old son, Brock, into the living room and clearly communicated the danger to him.

"Son, this stove is very, very hot. If you or anyone else touches it, they will get burned. See this brick? This is very easy to trip over. We do not want you to run anywhere in this living room because we don't want you to get hurt. We don't want you to accidently bump into Aunt Erin and the baby or anyone else, just in case they are close enough to get bumped into this stove. Is this clear, son?"

Brock nodded *yes*. So we did what we always did: We had him verbalize the rule so we could make sure he understood our directions.

"Brock, can you tell me what I just told you?"

"No running in the living room. The stove is hot and someone might get burned."

"That's right, honey."

The morning went very well, but the closer we got to naptime the rowdier Brock became. He began running laps through the dining room, down the hall, and then through the living room.

We gave him one reminder and had him repeat the rule verbally to make sure he understood. But just seconds later he had continued the disobedient running. At that point, I picked him up and carried him into the bedroom. I got down at his level and said, "Brock, what did we say about running around the stove?"

"Don't do it?"

"Yes, that's right. Did you run?"

He immediately nodded *yes* and began to cry.

"Was it wrong to disobey Mommy and Daddy?"

He nodded and eked out a *yes*.

"What could have happened because you ran and disobeyed?"

"The baby could have been burned."

"That's right. And it would have been bad if that happened, right, son?" Brock nodded in the affirmative with big crocodile tears running down his cheek. "You could have been burned and really gotten hurt too. Mommy and Daddy don't want you to get burned like that. God has placed us here as your mommy and daddy to protect you. To remind you how important it is that you listen and obey, Mommy is going to have to give you a spanking. Turn around."

He complied and I gave him a little swat over his padded behind. I gave him a big hug and said, "Honey, I love you and I want to keep you safe. Let's pray and ask God to help you obey, okay? I will pray first then you can talk to God and say anything you want."

I prayed, and then Brock spoke up. "Jesus, I am sorry I ran and didn't obey. Please help me obey. Thank you that baby Bekah didn't get burned."

Then I gave Brock a hug, and he smiled and said, "Thanks, Mom. I needed that spanking!"

Usually the thank-you for applying discipline comes much later— like when your kids have kids of their own! And years later, our son shared this same funny, "Thanks, I needed that" story during a speaking engagement with his father at a church worship service near the time of Brock's high school graduation. Brock said, "One of the things I appreciate about the way I was raised is that my parents disciplined me. When they said *no*, they meant it. They disciplined me so I could learn self-discipline. I go to public high school and a majority of my classmates have not been able to accomplish their hopes and dreams because they lack the discipline it takes to reach their goals. But I was fortunate to have parents who cared enough to apply discipline so I learned to discipline my time, my priorities, and my life to achieve the dreams God placed on my heart."

The question your toddler or your preschooler may or may not ask aloud (but they will be thinking!) is, "Mommy, Daddy, do you love me?" Having a plan for developing their character and their inner self-discipline is a powerful gift of love!

The Honor of Guarding Your Treasure

For most of you reading this book, being a watchman and your child's hero is not a burden, but rather an honor. You may respond much like most of the men and women in uniform do when we thank them for their military service: "Thank you. It is an honor."

It is an honor serving God and our children, because God has made them a treasure! God said to Israel, "For you are a people holy to the LORD your God. The LORD your God has chosen you out of all the peoples on the face of the earth to be his people, his treasured possession" (Deuteronomy 7:6).

And there's more! God extended this picture of you and your children being chosen and a priceless treasure to Him:

> For we know, brothers and sisters loved by God, that he has chosen you, because our gospel came to you not simply with words but also with power, with the Holy Spirit and deep conviction (1 Thessalonians 1:4-5).

> But you are a chosen people, a royal priesthood, a holy nation, God's special possession, that you may declare the praises of him who called you out of darkness into his wonderful light. Once you were not a people, but now you are the people of God; once you had not received mercy, but now you have received mercy (1 Peter 2:9-10).

Chosen for Greatness

Because you are God's chosen treasure, you make the wise choice to stand watch over your life. Your children are God's treasure, so your goal as a parent must be to guard your precious children and teach them how to stand guard over their own lives. In the teen years comes a changing of the guard. Eventually, you'll have to hand the responsibility over to your teen or young adult to "own." Your son or daughter will have to take full responsibility for his or her life and value himself or herself as God's chosen treasure. You guard the treasure early on and train your children to learn day after day, heaping skill upon skill, so that one day they will stand guard over the treasure of their own lives, values, and beliefs.

So what is the essence of the treasure that is so valuable—the treasure that will set your son or daughter up for a lifetime of success in life and love? You are standing guard over the core values that need to be developed in your son or daughter that will help him or her make wise choices. And because of the focus of this book, these core values and your child's ability to live them out will eventually bless their intimate life in marriage.

Remember, you will be teaching them there are two ways to live: You can do it the hard way or you can do it the smart way. If a child holds on to his or her core values as he or she develops, the teen years will be easier and you will have less drama and trauma. (Notice we said *less* rather than *no* drama and trauma! All teens have some.) And eventually, if your child grasps that he or she is a treasure, those core values will lead him or her to the wise relationship choices that will bring these verses to pass:

> I have come that they may have life, and have it to the full (John 10:10).

> "For I know the plans I have for you," declares the LORD, "plans to prosper you and not to harm you, plans to give you hope and a future" (Jeremiah 29:11).

All those teachable moments, times of discipline, and even sexual education instruction will be aimed at developing the character that will carry your child forward to the abundant life God has waiting. One of our favorite quotations from a parent came from the chaplain of the Superbowl-winning Indianapolis Colts, Ken Johnson. He told his children, "May your character keep you where your talent can take you."[1] Your children have gifts, talents and skills—but character is what will keep excellent opportunities coming their way.

Character Counts!

In this world we all can easily name hundreds of talented, powerful, successful, capable leaders in sports, business, politics, and even the church who didn't watch over their inner character or sexual decisions…and their errors splashed the tabloid headlines. You probably remember…

- the homosexual affair of megachurch pastor and then-President of the National Association of Evangelicals, Ted Haggard

- the "sexting" of newlywed Senator Anthony Weiner, betraying the trust of his pregnant wife and his constituents

- the disgrace of the Oval Office by President Clinton, who had oral sex with intern Monica Lewinsky

- the affair of South Carolina Governor Mark Sanford, who voted for the impeachment of Clinton following the Lewinsky scandal, declaring Clinton's behavior to be "reprehensible," yet, within a few years, abandoned his wife and children for a secret love affair with a woman from Argentina

- Kim Kardashian's extremely short 72-day marriage and subsequent one year (and counting) divorce proceeding

- the domestic violence of music icon Chris Brown toward girlfriend Rihanna

- Whitney Houston's on-again, off-again relationship with Bobby Brown. Whitney, a proclaimed Christian, struggled with drug addictions which ultimately led to her death in a hotel bathroom.

- golf legend Tiger Woods cheating with multiple mistresses, including waitresses, models, and porn stars

- basketball star Shawn Kemp fathering seven children out of wedlock

- General David Petraeus's resignation as director of the CIA due to an affair

- Coach Jerry Sandusky's conviction for multiple counts of child sexual abuse

- Governor Arnold Schwarzenegger fathering a child with his housekeeper

- Presidential candidate John Edwards cheating on his wife, Elizabeth, as she was dying of cancer

Sin leaves a wake of destroyed relationships, destroyed lives, and destroyed opportunities. Each one of these cases could have been avoided had those involved shown a little more character. If all these people had just listened to that inner compass that God places inside each person at creation, their personal lives would not be in shambles and their public reputations would have remained intact.

But for the Grace of God

If we think it can only happen to "those people," look in the mirror. We are all born with a sin nature:

> There is no one righteous, not even one; there is no one who understands; there is no one who seeks God. All have turned away, they have together become worthless; there is no one who does good, not even one (Romans 3:10-12).

But God has placed a conscience in us. We have the choice each day to listen—or not. Much like a shortwave radio can receive incoming dispatches from the police and emergency services, our heart is set to receive direction from God. He created our ears to hear and our heart to respond to his light: "For God, who said, 'Let light shine out of darkness,' made his light shine in our hearts to give us the light of the knowledge of God's glory displayed in the face of Christ" (2 Corinthians 4:6).

Character tunes us into God's voice, and our goal is to have our kids echo this sentiment as their own: "I desire to do your will, my God; your law is within my heart" (Psalm 40:8).

We each have the ability to hear from God, but in our world, many have simply decided to turn off their receiver. Our goal as parents is to train our kids to keep their "God receiver" on and tuned in to His frequency for living life. When our children are young, we help pattern their hearts to choose goodness, righteousness, and wisdom automatically. Our goal is to help them get into a habit of obeying us and God without question. Then as they get older, we help them learn how to apply God's Word and link it to their own thinking, logic, and long-range planning to design a life to look forward to living. We want them to elect to live the obedient life, surrendered to God for themselves. Our goal is to complete the baton handoff:

> Posterity will serve him; future generations will be told about the Lord. They will proclaim his righteousness, declaring to a people yet unborn: He has done it! (Psalm 22:30-31).

Teach Them to MIND You and MIND God

How do you instill obedience in your children? When you boil down this complex act, four strands form the cord of obedience to authority:

Model a legitimate authority

Instruct, clearly expecting obedience

Navigate follow-through

Develop a relationship

All four of these traits will help your child learn to desire obedience—but it takes *all* of them.

Model a Legitimate Authority

It is vital to model being a legitimate authority because you are your child's conduit to God. If your child can't obey you, how will he or she ever learn to follow God? You are their link, their instructor, their mentor and model. Your own integrity matters. It is confusing for children at any age to witness a parent's lack of judgment or bad behavior.

Bill and I know this firsthand. I (Pam) never knew when to obey my dad because a large majority of time he was drunk. See how my vision of God the Father was blurred at an early age? I (Bill) had a similar dilemma as my mother struggled with mental illness but refused help. She vacillated between anger, depression, paranoia, and complete withdrawal from life. She was supposed to be my model for trusting authority, but she was not very trustworthy. Your first step in helping your child obey you is to ask, "How well am I obeying God?"

Is there a habit He has asked you to stop? A behavior He has wanted you to seek help for? Your daily desire to please your main authority, God, will be the biggest influence on your child's ability to do the same.

Instruct, Clearly Expecting Obedience

Your child cannot obey an instruction he or she doesn't understand. Give instructions on any task clearly.

This ensures your child clearly understands what you are instructing him or her to do. This method can be used for the simplest tasks: putting toys away, making a bed, getting dressed, and hanging up clothes. The tasks will get increasingly complex as your child grows older, but the method will remain the same.

Navigate Follow-through

You can't reason with a two-year-old. So early on, you will have to impose discipline. For example, at fourteen months our oldest kept climbing on top of a glass end table—and jumping! I (Pam) wanted to avoid the catastrophe of broken glass, cuts, and bleeding so I would take him down and tell him, "No!"

Then I would place him away from the table in a toddler chair, and distract him with a different toy. I had to do this over and over and *over*. Each time, I would accompany the move with a stern "No!" Then I moved the chair further and further from the tempting table until he was in another room! But he did learn!

As your children get a little older they'll be asking, pleading, cajoling, and begging you for some activity, toy, or special privilege. We encourage you to mean "No!" when you say "No!" Don't let their whining, complaining, emotional outbursts wear you down. "No!" needs to mean "No!"

Dr. Tim Elmore explains the benefits of the word *no* in his book *Artificial Maturity:*

- Hearing the word "no" actually may force me toward a better alternative.

- Hearing the word "no" may save me from harm that I am prone to inflict on myself if I get my own way all the time.

- Hearing the word "no" actually prepares me for the real world, which often uses this word.

- Hearing the word "no" may build discipline inside of me that I would never develop if I simply heard the word "yes."

- Hearing the word "no" fosters creativity inside of me, as I must look for other solutions than the easy one I came up with the first time.[2]

No might bring tears today, but may save tears tomorrow.

Develop a Relationship

The most important ingredient in all this is your relationship with your child. The closer your child feels to you, the more he or she will want to please you. The stories you read, the time spent playing dress-up, playing with dolls or trucks, the family picnics, campouts, vacations, the bedtime prayers, the laughing around the dinner table, attending church as a family—all these things and more create an environment of trust. If your child feels you love her, then she will trust what you say more. He or she will know you have their best interests in mind, even if the choice is a difficult one for them to follow.

This bond will be attacked from the outside by society and from the inside by your own teen as he or she matures and wants to take ownership of his or her life. Eventually, if you do your part well and release them at natural intervals, your teen will make wise choices and take ownership and responsibility for his or her life. Your close bond will not just survive but become a lifelong, cherished relationship between you and your child.

Answers to Have Ready

In our own family, we cultivated this relationship bond and instilled a desire to obey in two ways: formally and informally.

Formal: In our book *The 10 Best Decisions a Parent Can Make*, we detail our parenting philosophy, tools and methods, so we won't share all the details here. We will, however, share the core tradition that became the foundation of our family, building a strong home and strong leaders at each stage of their lives growing up. Today, those sons are strong adult leaders and followers of Jesus. We call this core tradition *Learner and Leader Day*.

When Brock was a baby and we were in youth ministry, we looked around at the kids who were doing well in the youth group and noted they had certain character qualities, leadership traits, and life skills. The long list seemed to fall into three main categories:

First, *they loved God.* We wanted our own children to develop their own relationship with Jesus.

Second, *they loved to learn.* We wanted our children to have teachable attitudes.

Finally, *they were leaders.* We wanted our children to lead within their own personality styles and find their passion in life.

We decided the best way to instill character in our children was to have a fun family day—a Learner and Leader Day! On a Learner and Leader Day we would give new responsibilities and privileges to each child for the coming year, ask them to focus on a certain leadership trait, and present them with a gift and blessing to applaud God's strength and calling in their lives.

We have a set of criteria in choosing the gift:

- It must be *practical,* something I might have to buy anyway.

- It must be *personal.* The child should be able to tell I thought about the gift.

- It must be *prophetic,* meaning that it speaks the truth about the uniqueness, the calling, or the strength we see God building into each child.

On the Learner and Leader contract we also detailed the consequences for not keeping the contract. In their tween years, the children began to set their own consequences, thus owning their own lives. When they hit their teen years a set of new "contract" traditions are added, which we will talk about in future chapters.

Informal: We always shared a fun family day on Learner and Leader Day. It could be anything from a simple and inexpensive day at the beach or a picnic at the lake to something we had saved for, like a day at an amusement park. The day had to contain two components: fun as a family and individual one-on-one time with each child so we could talk through the coming year, share the key leadership trait we would be focusing on, and negotiate the privileges and responsibility chart. Then we gave each child a gift and a prayer.

We want our children to elect to live the obedient life, surrendered to God for themselves. Our goal is to complete the baton handoff:

> Posterity will serve him; future generations will be told about the Lord. They will proclaim his righteousness, declaring to a people yet unborn: He has done it! (Psalm 22:30-31).

Parent to Parent

Speaking of obedience, adults also have to look at themselves in the mirror and answer the question, "Have I obeyed God in this area of sexuality?"

Let's first look at why so many people have *not* chosen it for themselves (perhaps you might also fall into this category). For those who have not elected to remain pure before marriage, it could be because they lacked...

Information

They do not know premarital sex is wrong. They missed hearing the biblical truths and God's view on the topic of sex. Tell them all that you know about God's view, buy them their own copy of this book, take them to seminars on the topic, give them radio ministry programs, podcasts or audio resources to inform them; invite them to your church, offer to do a Bible study. Give them website links, videos, or other media to connect them to more and more of God's truth. As you help them fill in the blanks, these parents are often very excited to give their children better opportunities to live out God's plan for their lives.

Desperation

Some people were so desperate for love that they gave in to temptation, hoping it would give them that love they craved. Often these people came from homes filled with pain, chaos, confusion, and dysfunction. They may have baggage to unpack, and professional counseling ministries like Celebrate Recovery or small group Bible studies dealing with overcoming your past are all helpful tools. Those seeking to gain victory over their desperate need for love need to trade in false expressions of love for true expressions of God's love. Often these people are filled with shame or guilt because deep down they knew sex was a compromise...and they came out on the short end of the deal.

You may want to share verses with these people about God's forgiveness, redemption, and ability to renew a life through His gift of salvation. Ask these people to make the choice to accept His offer of mercy and forgiveness. This means confessing their sin and simply acknowledging that their premarital sex was a sin, but one that God will forgive if they will come to Him. These parents are often very motivated to save their own children some of the pain they experienced and will help them avoid carrying their sin on to the next generation.

Rebellion

These people can be the hardest to share your convictions with. They defend their right to have premarital sex and, even if they are parents now, if single, they may still be actively rebelling against God's plan for love. They might accuse you of being old-fashioned, out of touch, or a prude. Look beyond their name-calling to their path. You now know what is ahead for them if they are still sexually active outside marriage, and you know what is ahead for their children if they maintain their casual view toward sex.

Try to withhold judgment toward these parents and share with them information on *why* you have made your choices and decisions about parenting. Unfold God's view in small bits, as they are willing to listen. If they're willing, build a relationship with these families and offer to connect their children to wholesome activities. As they see the difference in your life and your family, their misconceptions may fall by the wayside and they will become open to hearing more about God's plan for themselves and their children. When these parents do have a paradigm shift, they are often able to harness all their rebellious energy toward the passions of God's heart.

Exasperation

Some people just gave up. They might have known and believed sex before marriage was not God's plan for their lives. They might not have been rebellious and may even have been someone others would have been surprised to know engaged in premarital sex. They might have simply let down their guard, little by little, slowly. Perhaps they gave away their virginity in a long-term dating relationship or during engagement. They might have felt alone in their convictions to hold on to their purity, perhaps even ridiculed for their virginity, so eventually they just compromised their beliefs. Some people just wave the white flag and give up! These parents usually need help forgiving themselves, and then help believing it can be different for their children. By offering these parents tangible hope and help and connecting their children to opportunities for spiritual growth and healthy church or parent-led sex education, their children can find a different path from their parents'.

What you might notice missing here is the loss of virginity through rape or sexual abuse. In these cases, we believe God sees the victim not as someone who gave away her gift, but rather someone from whom it was robbed or stolen. Later in the book we will deal more with these cases and how to handle them but, for now, if this is your story, trust that God sees your pain and He holds the perpetrator accountable for the loss, not you. (See Deuteronomy 22:25-27. God gave rapists the death penalty and the victim was freed to move forward with her life with her family's help.)

As your children grow, you will need to be able to defend a biblical view of abstinence until marriage. It might help to start with the myriad of reasons people have not elected to choose God's best in their lives. Some of the above reasons should elicit a feeling of compassion—even for the most rebellious and selfish. Try to remember that these people are not the enemy. Satan is the enemy, and he has them trapped in sin. As the apostle Paul puts it, "our struggle is not against flesh and blood, but against the rulers, against the authorities, against the powers of this dark world and against the spiritual forces of evil in the heavenly realms" (Ephesians 6:12). You will be more effective in persuading others, including your own children, if you keep the truth about the real enemy in mind.

Answers for Your Heart

Remember to grab your own journal and pray through your own past and feelings about it. Then you will be better able to talk with other parents and your own children. In your journal write the answers to these questions:

- God, the reason I did or didn't choose to remain pure before marriage was:
- My biggest fear for my own child is:
- My biggest fear about talking to others about my beliefs and values in this area of sexuality is:

The book of 1 John teaches much on love. Set aside time to read the entire five-chapter book, noting these verses in particular:

> If we confess our sins, he is faithful and just and will forgive us our sins and purify us from all unrighteousness (1 John 1:9).

> If anyone acknowledges that Jesus is the Son of God, God lives in them and they in God. And so we know and rely on the love God has for us. God is love. Whoever lives in love lives in God, and God in them. This is how love is made complete among us so that we will have confidence on the day of judgment: In this world we are like Jesus. There is no fear in love. But perfect love drives out fear, because fear has to do with punishment. The one who fears is not made perfect in love. We love because he first loved us (1 John 4:15-19).

In your journal, write down any other verses that were encouraging to your heart and life.

Can You Help Me Become SMART?

The one who gets wisdom loves life; the one who
cherishes understanding will soon prosper.

Proverbs 19:8

Okay, confession time. How many of you have a "My kid is smarter than your kid" bumper sticker on your car? You know, the ones schools give out for honor roll. Is it proudly displayed for everyone in the Wal-Mart parking lot and gridlock traffic to see?

Some people get a little attitude toward us parents who want our kids to be smart...and it can be reflected in their bumper stickers:

My parrot can talk. Can your honor student fly?
My kid can beat up your honor student!
My child is an honor student at the state correctional facility.
If that kid is an honor student, he must not really be yours.
My daughter can out-fish your honor student.
Previous owner had an honor student!

People might joke about their kid being smart—or not so smart. But deep down, all parents—all *good* parents—want their children to be wise, discerning, and yes, smart enough to make right choices that lead to happiness and God's favor and blessing over their lives.

Because our goal as parents is to help our kids be smart in a sexually-saturated world, let's look at the five core character development areas and link them as an acrostic. We all want our children, teens, and young adults to make S.M.A.R.T. decisions. We hope, pray, and train so they will:

Suspend gratification: the ability to delay indulging desires.

Mind authority: a longing to obey and please God above all others.

Adore God: cultivate a listening heart.

Resolve to be authentic: be genuine, real, and honest.

Trust the trustworthy: the ability to relax in a safe environment.

Let's take a closer look at each one to see why each is important, especially in the area of your child's future marriage and sexuality, and how to cultivate each trait in your child's heart and life.

Suspend Gratification

As the mom or dad of a preschooler, you were painfully aware of the daily testing of your patience. Your child had no patience! The good news is that all the "Please Mommy, please Daddy! I neeeeeeeeed it!" pleas are the forum for cultivating your child's ability to wait, to delay gratification, and (ultimately) to teach them to defer their sexual desires until the day they say, "I do."

We know God values delayed gratification because the words *wait, waited,* and *waiting* are so prevalent in the Bible. Often the waiting is linked to a payoff. Waiting is a priority with God, and waiting gives us all kinds of splendid blessings, including heaven and being rewarded for walking faithfully with Jesus. So our goal is to help our kids grasp that waiting brings with it a cool, awesome, rewarded value!

Waiting for the *I Do*

If waiting is so important, how can we help our kids learn to wait for the best and not settle? Give me a minute…and we will tell you… in a little while…See, you don't like waiting much either! But when

God says it's not time yet, it's good to wait. And if God's Word says it is His will for sex to come after the "I do," we are to wait until *after* the marriage ceremony for sex. Here is one passage that captures the priority of waiting for sexual intimacy until after the wedding day (more verses will be handled later—so wait!):

> It is God's will that you should be sanctified: that you should avoid sexual immorality; that each of you should learn to control your own body in a way that is holy and honorable, not in passionate lust like the pagans, who do not know God; and that in this matter no one should wrong or take advantage of a brother or sister. The Lord will punish all those who commit such sins, as we told you and warned you before. For God did not call us to be impure, but to live a holy life. Therefore, anyone who rejects this instruction does not reject a human being but God, the very God who gives you his Holy Spirit (1 Thessalonians 4:3-8).

Since this passage is one of the core reasons for writing this entire book, let's take a closer look at the key words. We have written this as an expanded paragraph, adding biblical word definitions in parentheses to gain a clearer understanding of God's heart and intent in asking this of every person:

It is God's will *(His desire, decision, and intent)* that you should be sanctified *(consecrated, set apart for a holy use)*: that you should avoid *(abstain, distance yourself, keep away from)* sexual immorality *(fornication [consenting sex involving someone who is unmarried], all sex of any kind outside the context of the marital bed, adultery, premarital and extramarital intercourse, homosexuality, prostitution, and other perversions)*; that each of you should learn *(know, realize, be aware of, recognize, and have the information)* to control *(acquire and possess)* your own body in a way that is holy *(consecrated, dedicated to God)* and honorable *(respectful and treating it as if it has high, precious value)*, not in passionate lust *(passion that leads to a craving, deep desire, or lust)* like the pagans, who do not know God *(who do not believe in God, or have yet to realize or perceive God)*; and that in this matter no one should wrong *(go beyond, trespass, or step over)* or take advantage *(exploit or outwit because of a motivation of greed or self-indulgence)* of a brother or sister. The Lord will punish *(judge, avenge, and bestow His wrath on)* all those who commit such sins *(become an adulterer)*, as we told you *(testified, admonished, instructed)* and warned *(predicted; told of some future happening that is dangerous and may lead to serious consequence)* you before. For God did not call us to be impure *(morally or physically unclean in a way that defiles the soul by all kinds of wrongdoing or sexual profligacy [extravagance, wasteful, reckless, licentious, wicked, or immoral behavior])*, but to live a holy life *(consecrated and dedicated to God)*. Therefore, anyone who rejects *(refuses to accept, consider, or submit to; or who nullifies or regards as nothing)* this instruction *(education, direction, or showing the way)* does not reject a human being but God, the very God who gives you his Holy Spirit *(The Holy Yahweh, The Supreme Creator and Sustainer of the universe)*.

A Splash of Ice-Cold Water

When we read this the first time, it felt like a bucket of ice-cold water had been thrown over us on a freezing cold snowy day. It stopped us in our tracks and took our breath away. I (Pam) had attended church on and off for most of my growing-up years and only a few mentions had ever been made concerning God's will for us to wait until marriage for sex. I never remember a sermon on this set of verses until I was in college at a Campus Crusade for Christ leadership conference. Bill had even less exposure to God's Word, but he, too, was at this same leadership conference. We were not yet dating; in fact, it was at this conference that we first met. God wanted to make sure we both heard this information loud and clear!

Most of society carries little or no regard for casual sex, but that doesn't mean that an apathetic attitude toward God's plan for sex is right, healthy, or smart. God is very specific in what He is asking and equally specific in painting a word picture of the consequences of disobedience. When I (Bill) became a pastor, I was committed to preaching through the entire Bible, word by word, so all of the heart of God would be heard by those I was responsible for leading—not just the happy verses that are easy to hear and quote, but *all* the verses! It is when we see God in His many facets that life, His commands, and His promises finally make sense.

Why God Says *Wait*

God is not a killjoy. In fact, He's just the opposite: a joy-creator. You saw in chapter one that God has several really wonderful purposes for sex and that sex is a gift—one of His most creative gifts, which brings humankind joy, pleasure, and happiness. But it is only within its proper context (a committed, faithful marriage) that sex can be all it was created to be. When we are wholly committed, we are *holy* and He is *committed* to bring us blessing and joy.

Outside these boundaries, sex has natural consequences that we believe are a part of God avenging and releasing His wrath: disease, physical pain, shame, complicated relationships, distrust, a difficult life path, unplanned pregnancy, the guilt of an abortion, consequences that affect future fertility, less money to live on because you are supporting your offspring, broken hearts, broken lives, broken hopes, broken dreams—the consequences are many and varied. A few minutes of thrill (or, for many, no thrill) cannot possibly be worth so many of these harsh consequences. And we are *sure* that death from HIV/AIDS is not worth the rush that might have been felt from sex outside the context of marriage.

Why would God ordain such a strong restriction on our sex drives? Because premarital sex…

- keeps us from being consecrated or dedicated to God. It places our will above God's will.

- exposes us to more sex, riskier sex, and more uncommitted sex. Sex ignited outside marriage lights the fire of more forbidden fruit, which can endanger our hearts, health, and life. The desire for the forbidden can, in turn, rob from future marital sex, as it becomes harder to reach orgasm unless we are engaged in the illicit or forbidden. It can also become hard to be satisfied by just one lover and it lessens our ability to be faithful after marriage.

• lowers our view of ourselves as holy, treasured, and valuable. God holds sex as a treasure to give to a precious individual, and we devalue it and ourselves when we misuse it. A consistent misuse of the gift of sex will slowly erode a person's self-esteem. Each sexual interaction can be like leaving a piece of yourself behind until none of your authentic self is left.

• lessens our ability to impose self-control or self-discipline. Lack of self-control can easily seep over to other areas of life, and an undisciplined life can unravel God's best plan for our lives.

• creates a selfish attitude so that sex becomes more about what you can *get* than what you can *give*. Traits God says premarital sex produces are a desire to go beyond what your partner might be comfortable with, a willingness to trespass or step over others to get your way, and a desire to take advantage of, exploit, or outwit someone to indulge your own greedy desires.

• reduces our ability to stop sinning. People become accustomed to sexual profligacy: extravagance of time, money, or effort given just for a sexual thrill, a wasteful or short-term view of life, reckless endangerment in pursuit of desire, licentious, wicked, or escalating immoral behaviors in search of the next sexual high.

• trains people to ignore God and God's instructions. It becomes easier and easier to stray from God and shut down His voice and calling in life.

• unleashes God's wrath. Premarital sex opens a person up to Satan's realm. In the days of the early church, when the Scripture we just studied was written, sex was woven into the sacred rituals of many pagan religions. Temples employed prostitutes of both genders and an atmosphere of hedonism, or self-gratification, reigned. Immorality was everywhere as people indulged themselves in the pursuit of pleasure.

To refute or rebuff God's plan is to open oneself up to a foothold placed in your life—either willingly and with full knowledge or unwillingly. Remember, Satan is a deceiver; he sneaks in any way he can and loves to wreck and ruin a life. That's why we're reminded, "Be alert and of sober mind. Your enemy the devil prowls around like a roaring lion looking for someone to devour" (1 Peter 5:8).

But God gives the solution to overcoming Satan's temptations and attacks in this same passage. To the above warnings He adds:

> Resist him, standing firm in the faith, because you know that the family of believers throughout the world is undergoing the same kind of sufferings. And the God of all grace, who called you to his eternal glory in Christ, after you have suffered a little while, will himself restore you and make you strong, firm and steadfast (1 Peter 5:9-10).

Waiting for Marshmallows

Having sensed God's heart for sex, let's be willing to walk that heart back to the first ABC's or building blocks of a child's life. A simple way to begin training a child to wait for something vital and important, like sex in marriage, is to first equip him or her to wait for the small things. For example, as he or she begins snacking, space the snacks out at regular healthy intervals (you can consult your pediatrician or a certified nutritionist on this). Even having a preschooler or elementary child wait a few minutes for his appetite to be fulfilled helps train him to understand that there is a reward for waiting patiently. If he wants a treat (ice cream, for example) and you decide it's appropriate, he will have to wait patiently for it. If he whines, start the timer and make him wait all over, this time without whining. When the toddler picks up toys and places them in the toy box, offer a reward—a snack, reading his favorite book, or a trip to the park. Teach your preschooler that rewards come *after* the work. And when she sees a toy on TV that she wants, make her do simple chores to earn it. Parents who run right out and indulge their preschooler's every whim are setting themselves up for a world of hurt later. Being accustomed to instant indulgence will make your teen the one who pressures his or her date to "put out" just like he or she is pressuring you to jump and fulfill every desire!

In the early seventies a professor at Stanford University, Walter Mischel, tested the willpower of four-year-old children in a famous experiment. He put them in a room and placed a large marshmallow on a table close to them. He told them that they could eat the marshmallow right away if they wanted, but if they waited to eat it for 15 minutes, he would give them a *second* marshmallow. He left the room and observed the results through a two-way mirror. The results? Some children grabbed the marshmallow and ate it right away. Some tried to wait, but could only hold out for a few minutes before succumbing to temptation. Only 30 percent were able to wait the whole 15 minutes for the promised reward.

Later, when the children had entered high school, the researchers caught up with them. The children were examined for the capacity to plan, think ahead, find solutions to problems, and interact well with their peers. The results were startling. The differences researchers had observed between the students 14 years earlier were excellent predictors of the children's behavior in high school. The children who were able to wait instead of gobbling up the marshmallow generally had a more positive outlook, were self-motivating, and had developed healthy habits that pointed toward future success. The children who *couldn't* wait for a second marshmallow struggled in stressful situations, were more likely to have behavioral problems, and had trouble maintaining friendships. The children who were able to wait had, on average, an SAT score that was *two hundred ten points higher* than their peers who could only wait thirty seconds.[1]

Our society is one where no one wants to wait for sex, save for expenditures, or plan for things like vacations—or even calorie control! Our instant gratification society is killing us.

Building a Waiting Priority

From the time our sons had the ability to reach up and demand with an "Ugh! Ugh!" we taught them that *patient* means "Willing to wait." We rewarded them anytime they waited patiently, saying, "Thank you, honey; you are waiting so nicely." We even taught them the song about Herbert the Snail learning patience!

Later we'll talk about other things we did to help our own children wait for the best in life and love. For now, take our word for it, this work early in your child's life is worth it! But it can be tough to maintain. Chances are you have had those moments at the checkout stand when your little one wants all the gum, candy, and other treats so shrewdly placed at toddler eye-level, knowing the kids will whine and the majority of parents will simply give in, creating profit for the store.

One of our friends had an all-out showdown with his first grader who wanted a toy. He calmly said, "Not today, honey," but then the inner Tasmanian devil took over and it was an all-out screaming fit on Aisle 10! He ultimately picked up his daughter and carried her out of the store, ending their shopping trip. She had been yelling things like "Why Daddy? I want it Daddy! Yes, Daddy!" But when he picked her up and carried her to the car she screamed, "Someone help me! This is not my daddy!" Fortunately it was a small town, and the dad had plenty of family pictures and a few good neighbors to vouch for his identity and family connections! We share this extreme example so that the next time your child begins her pouting, his stomping, her screaming, or his temper tantrum, you will know it can be worse. It can definitely be worse because a spoiled child becomes a demanding teen and evolves into an impatient date who wants sex when he or she wants it, how he or she wants it—*now!* Helping your daughter parent a child while she's still in high school or hiring a lawyer to defend your son against date rape is harder than saying no at the checkout counter!

Even if your child is older, a middle schooler, or in senior high, having him or her earn the extras he or she wants will help develop the delayed-gratification muscle. And be careful with lavish parties and gifts. If your child takes a limo to the sixth grade graduation party or has a sweet sixteen as extravagant as many people's weddings, he or she will feel entitled. An attitude of entitlement only serves to erode the delayed-gratification character you are seeking to build. Decisions like saving for his or her first car, that gaming unit, or even church summer camp will help develop the character needed to make wiser relationship choices later.

Next time, remember: It really isn't about giving the candy bar, the designer jeans, or the coolest new computer. It is about your child's future! Your ability to hold the line helps your child succeed later in life. Leadership expert John Maxwell explains that "timing is everything." *When* we make a move is often as important as *what* move we make:

> The wrong action at the wrong time leads to disaster. The right action at the wrong time brings resistance. The wrong action at the wrong time is a mistake. The right action at the right time results in success.[2]

Helping your child learn this, by first modeling it and then holding him or her to a waiting lifestyle, will be their first step toward success.

Mind Authority

We all love those obedient children. Who doesn't adore the preschooler who stands next to his parents and patiently waits to be acknowledged? We love to hear, "Yes, Mommy. Yes, Daddy." We like to look good as parents when our children obey, but that shouldn't be our primary motivation. Rather, obedience should be vital because it is how children learn to be obedient to God.

We encourage you to continue to be a legitimate authority in your child's life. Two critical choices on your part will better ensure wisdom on your child's part all along his or her growing-up path.

First, maintain your own integrity. When we were in youth ministry, we could almost predict a teen's implosion if his or her parents divorced or one of them had an affair. One father with several teen-aged children—a man who had held himself up as a Christian leader—decided to come out of the closet and make his homosexual lifestyle public. Bill begged him to turn back from this choice, but the man felt he needed to be "authentic."

He told Bill, "I have denied my feelings too long. It is my turn for happiness." Bill, seeing he was losing the battle with this self-centered dad, said, "Can you at least put off the decision until your kids are in college or young adults? Give them a chance to be solid in their own life and sexuality before cracking their world wide open."

The father's reply was, "My lover won't wait and neither will I."

Change the scenario to a heterosexual affair and the hurt is just the same. We have seen both mothers and fathers place their sex lives ahead of the well-being of their own children and futures. This is the height of selfishness. (If you have already had a breach of integrity, stay tuned—we'll talk more about how to handle this later. But for now, Mom and Dad, stay the course of obeying God too!) As a parent, you decided to give birth to your child. Now see it through! From this moment forward, make all your choices with your child's best interest in mind!

Make the Commands Clear

When you give instructions to your child, make them clear. In our home, with any task or chore, we held to this series of instructions:

I do, you watch (so your child can clearly see, hear, and experience how to succeed).

We do it together (so your child can experience success with you—a relationship builder).

You do, I watch (so he or she can succeed and hear praise or fail with a safety net, thus learning from errors so they'll succeed next time).

You do alone (applause!).

It is all too easy to be angry or discipline a child for something that you, as a parent, have never really enabled him or her to do successfully. Be sure to be clear!

Adore God

To be SMART, your child will need to develop a personal relationship with God. In the chapters to come, you will see how a little proactive hard work can have impressive positive payoffs. But some of you might already feel shame or guilt for not having done things so proactively. God knew exactly when you would hear some of the truths in this book—trust His heart and His timing! God can take what you have built and add Himself to it. Even if your family's a dysfunctional one, try to cultivate a relationship with your child. At the right moment, it can be enough to help your teen make a wise choice.

My (Pam's) father struggled with alcoholism. The distance grew between us emotionally. However, my mother overcompensated and went out of her way to build strong bonds with me and my siblings. She was my Campfire Girl club leader, my 4-H club leader, my Vacation Bible School craft leader, my team mom, and my room mother. She tended my emotional well-being and soul. In the middle of a very chaotic and crazy home environment, I knew she always had my best in mind. While she regrets not reaching out for help for our family sooner (through a counselor or Alcoholics Anonymous), she did take us to church weekly. Even before she herself had a personal relationship with God she was looking out for ours.

Because of my strained relationship with my father, as a teen I was desperate for the love of a man. I was like many teen girls, where a few sweet words and a few kind gestures from a guy fooled me into thinking I was in love. If pressured, a battle raged inside me—should I please my boyfriend or please God and my mom? I was a young believer, and I did know God loved me, but at that stage of my life, as a teenager, it was my relationship with my mother that kept me from giving in to urges, pressures, and persuasive words that could have completely altered the course of my life and future.

My mom was already in enough pain because of my father's drinking; I couldn't do anything to cause her more pain. Having sex outside of marriage would have broken her heart, and a teen pregnancy would have as well. I thought she was committed to being pro-life, but I didn't ever want to put her in the situation of counseling me through that hard choice. Her love for me and my love for her was a safeguard on my future. I thank God every day for my mother's committed love because it gave me strength in fighting the demons of our dysfunctional home. It made me refuse to settle for less than God's best and pursue healing. Her love gave me the ability to receive God's love, and God's love led me to my amazing husband, Bill.

Be encouraged. Even in a less-than-perfect environment, God can meet you and teach you how to love lavishly…just the way He loves you. And that is the key to unlocking your child's ability to adore God—show her God adores her. Show him God loves him and has his back. When a child, a teen, a college student, or a young adult is fully convinced God loves her, it raises her ability to trust Him with her heart, relationships, and future.

Resolve to Be Authentic

It is imperative to instill the value of being genuine, real, and honest in our kids. Our children need to be honest with us so they can learn to be honest with themselves and with God. When we were in youth ministry and the pastorate, we had more than one student in our office who said the same thing: "We didn't mean for it to happen. We thought we could handle being alone (in an empty house, in the dark, together, in a sleeping bag)." *Seriously? You thought that was a good plan?*

We heard so many of these lame stories. An honest teen or young adult knows they would rarely succeed under those kinds of circumstances!

One young woman we know never went on a date with a young man she was interested in because she was afraid of what her parents would say about him because he was not a believer. But she didn't protect her life with good boundaries, and one day she discovered she was pregnant—to a guy she never went on a "date" with! If a conversation about his character qualities was hard before, it was next to impossible now! Her double life had serious implications!

Our children need to learn to be honest with us. We told our children, "There is nothing you can do that will ever make us stop loving you. If you make a mistake, come straight to us and confess, because if we hear it from you your punishment will be much less than if we hear it from anyone else." It is hard to hear our kids are less than perfect, but it is even more difficult to deal with someone who has lost his ability to tell the truth…or *see* the truth. Encourage honesty in all ways possible.

Trust the Trustworthy

We as parents should foster trust so our children gain the ability to relax in a safe environment. You might be wondering…Why is *resting in trust* one of the five core values? Why is it vital to learn to "chill out"? To truly have a remarkable sex life once married you need to be able to be completely open, vulnerable, and free. A woman must relax to reach orgasm. In fact, while researching our book *Red-Hot Monogamy*, we found a study that marked trust as the number-one factor that positively contributes to a woman's ability to climax.

As parents, we want to build a healthy boundary around sexuality—not an impenetrable fortress with an electric fence and razor wire! Some well-meaning parents use scare tactics and exclusively negative messages to keep their children away from sex, apparently thinking that somehow, on the child's honeymoon, the happy couple will suddenly be able to relax and enjoy sex. That's not the outcome of fear-based parenting. More than one solid Christian couple has shared with us the mental and emotional hurdle they had to overcome to replace the negative sexual messages their well-meaning parents gave to "protect" them.

Rather than reverting to fear tactics, instead model affection as normal and natural. Let your children see you hug, kiss, and flirt with your spouse. Appropriately express tenderness to your child as well. Let it be natural to cuddle, pat, or scratch his or her back, run your fingers through his curls, brush her hair, pat your child's hand, give a neck or shoulder massage, and give hugs and kisses. As your child transitions through his or her teen years, you will adjust how to handle affection toward him or her. Do not be afraid of tenderness and affection or your anxiety will be transferred to your child and he or she will have a difficult transition into marital sex.

Overall, verbalize and model the tenderness, affection, kindness, and physical expressions of feelings that are positive languages of love. Your view of love, sex, and marriage will color your child's.

Answers to Have Ready

Here are some verses to begin to share with your child, of any age, that describe the lavish, relentless love of God. You can communicate them to your child any way you like—just be creative! You might choose to read one aloud before each meal, pray one each night over your child at bedtime, print and pack it in his or her lunch, send it to him in a text, or post it on her door or mirror.

> For I am convinced that neither death nor life, neither angels nor demons, neither the present nor the future, nor any powers, neither height nor depth, nor anything else in all creation, will be able to separate us from the love of God that is in Christ Jesus our Lord (Romans 8:38-39).

> I have loved you with an everlasting love; I have drawn you with unfailing kindness (Jeremiah 31:3).

> But when the kindness and love of God our Savior appeared, he saved us, not because of righteous things we had done, but because of his mercy (Titus 3:4-5).

> "Because he loves me," says the LORD, "I will rescue him; I will protect him, for he acknowledges my name. He will call on me, and I will answer him; I will be with him in trouble, I will deliver him and honor him. With long life I will satisfy him and show him my salvation" (Psalm 91:14-16).

> The LORD is gracious and compassionate, slow to anger and rich in love. The LORD is good to all; he has compassion on all he has made (Psalm 145:8-9).

> "Though the mountains be shaken and the hills be removed, yet my unfailing love for you will not be shaken nor my covenant of peace be removed," says the LORD, who has compassion on you (Isaiah 54:10).

> Because of his great love for us, God, who is rich in mercy, made us alive with Christ even when we were dead in transgressions—it is by grace you have been saved (Ephesians 2:4-5).

> This is how we know what love is: Jesus Christ laid down his life for us (1 John 3:16).

Parent to Parent

One of the simplest tools we used to help our kids develop a strong inner compass was to teach them how to use their moral GPS. We taught our kids that before they said or did anything they were in question about, they should ask, "Does this show respect for *God, People,* and *Self?*"

Answers for Your Heart

Before God, ask, *What things in my past or in my thinking need to move to match up with Your view of love and sex? What can I do to help my child become SMART?* We will give you more opportunities to deal with your own baggage further into this book, but for now, ask yourself, *Does my child know that I love him? Am I balanced between discipline (the ability to say no and enforce it) and devotion (the ability to say yes to relationship builders and appropriate affection toward my child)?*

On the continuum below, mark the place you fall on the delicate balance of imposing discipline and expressing devotion.

Discipline   Devotion
I am harder on my child.   *I show love and affection.*

4

Where Do Babies Come From?

The goal of this command is love, which comes from a pure
heart and a good conscience and a sincere faith.

1 Timothy 1:5

Stephanie was getting ready to have the first "big talk" with her five-year-old daughter, Jeannie. She knew it was time to start satisfying her daughter's curiosity about the facts of life, but she didn't want to overdo it. She wanted to discern what Jeannie already knew first. Stephanie asked, "Honey, you know you were once in Mommy's tummy, right? Do you know where babies come from?"

Jeannie, wanting to accurately and politely answer her mother said, "Well Mom, I was in your tummy a long time ago so I don't really remember. Why don't you tell me about it? Refresh my memory."

It would sure be easier on all of us if our kids really *did* remember being born. There would be a lot less stress in our hearts over how much to tell them and when. They don't remember, however, and therefore God entrusted these innocent lives and inquisitive hearts to us so we could guide them in the discovery of the wonders of their bodies, the longings in their hearts, and the miracle of birth. We can't afford to punt on this privilege, Mom and Dad. It is vital that your children hear the right information from *you* because you are the safest, most trusted people in their lives!

SPEAK to Them

When it comes to talking about sexual development, what do little kids need from their parents? In simplest terms, they need parents who will SPEAK to them with:

Security

Progressive exposure

Explanations

Asking first

Keeping it simple

Security

Security is vital in the early years because it is the time in life when kids learn to bond. Through interaction with the significant adults in their lives, they learn to identify who is safe and who is to be avoided. They discover the strength of being emotionally attached to other human beings. They develop their basic understanding of how relationships are supposed to work. If your child feels bonded to you, he or she will embrace your guidance and develop healthier relational instincts. Children who feel disconnected or unsafe tend to be drawn to unhealthy choices when it comes to relationships. Speaking with your child about love and sex, therefore, begins with a secure environment that helps create a good inner compass and a sincere conscience.

There are a number of habits you can establish as a conscientious parent that will maximize your child's ability to bond with you in a healthy way:

- Develop routines: bath time, bedtime, breakfast time, naptime, playtime. A consistent rhythm in life is a security blanket to a baby and toddler.

- Create a safe home. A childproofed home provides freedom for your child to roam in a protected manner. You will find yourself saying *yes* more often than *no* if you simply create a home that is less of a showplace and more of a safe place.

- Provide a consistent caregiver. You two are the best care-givers since no one loves a child like a parent! If your work or finances will not allow one of you as a parent to be home during the day, a committed family member who is a talented caregiver is a close second! Nana, Papa, aunts, or uncles can be excellent choices. If a family member is not available, look in your neighborhood or church for a caregiver who is known for extraordinary love or care. The fewer hours a small baby or toddler can be in a large child-care facility, the easier bonding will be. Some workplaces offer an onsite childcare facility where you can drop in on your lunch hour and breaks. A few forward-thinking com-panies offer private office options for mothers with small sleeping babies that allow her to bring a newborn to work.

Secure with God

A child who believes that God's love is real and that He sees every-thing will make better choices in all areas of life. Confidence will grow in light of the fact that "God's love has been poured out into our hearts through the Holy Spirit" (Romans 5:5). Every decision will be tem-pered by the understanding that "His eyes are on the ways of mortals; he sees their every step" (Job 34:21). In fact, one of the names of God in the Old Testament is *El Roi*—"the God who sees." In Genesis 16:13, Hagar, feeling alone, fearful for her death, and fearful for the life of her child, was the first person to use this title: "She gave this name to the Lord who spoke to her: 'You are the God who sees me,' for she said, 'I have now seen the One who sees me.'"

Throughout the Bible, God's all-seeing nature is presented as one of the motivations for making healthy decisions in life. God sees all a child does—both the good and the disobedient actions—with eyes of love and righteousness. You should, therefore, communicate *both* sides of God's character—His judgment balanced with His grace. It is in the full picture of who God is that true security is found. As your child begins to comprehend that God is just, he will sense His protection against those who do evil or seek to hurt others. As your child learns that God is all-loving, she will find comfort in the fact that God rewards good decisions. This provides a secure environment for making wise choices that lead to a life of integrity.

Secure at Home

A secure home will help kids relax, think more clearly, discover their uniqueness, and explore social interaction. You can create a safe environment in a number of strategic areas:

Physical safety. Childproof your home with cabinet closures, drawer-pull catches, pool covers, and electrical socket covers installed. Door locks should be functioning properly while medicines, guns, and toxins should be secured away from curious little ones. Where appropriate, fences will help keep dangerous people and animals out and the child safely in the yard.

Emotional safety. Ample affirmations, loving hugs, kisses, and tender acts of appropriate affection will help your child feel emotionally safe. Yelling, demeaning speech, angry outbursts, swearing, and media that is not child appropriate should not have a place in your home and lifestyle.

Spiritual safety. Small habits such as saying grace, sharing goodnight prayers, and church attendance are good family routines to implement. The Bible, along with Christian children's videos and books, will layer in strong early roots to build a safety net around the heart of your child.

Relational safety. Be aware of who enters your home and seek to learn about the families of the children who live near you. Is there strife, a divorce, domestic violence, or inappropriate language or media in the homes of those children? Choices in the homes of friends, families, and neighbors will have an effect on yours. Be vigilant but not paranoid! There is no need to completely isolate yourselves. After all, your home may become the safe place for the children in your neighborhood!

Secure With Their Own Bodies

To build a secure foundation toward his or her body, seek to build a sense of awe. Linda and Richard Eyre, parents of nine children and authors of *Teaching Your Children Values*, remind us all as parents to not miss the wonder of creation:

> In dealing with young children, every available opportunity should be taken to point out how lucky we are to be able to see the beauties of the season, to hear creative and inspirational music, to taste different and unique combinations of food…to touch a baby's cheek or a kitten's soft fur, and especially to feel the love that we have for others in our family. The list of things to point out and be grateful for is endless. The more a child can appreciate his own body as a preschooler, the better foundation he will have for feeling positive about the greatest of all physical miracles.[1]

Our goal was to help our children be secure enough to know:

- My body is a gift
- My body is good
- My body is private
- My body is to be protected

Secure with Mom and Dad

Let your children hear the words, "I love you," "I am so proud of you," "I see how obedient you are being," "Our family is our priority," and, "Even when my work is difficult, my heart is with you!" often. Your young child was created to believe what you say about them during this bonding phase of life. Therefore, your words and actions of affirmation create a deep sense of security within them.

One of the best ways to build a secure foundation for your child's sexual future is to tell them the truth. We decided to be honest in all areas so that when we shared the truth in vital areas, our boys would believe us. So for us, there was a clear line between pretend and real.

Pretend were precious stories from children's literature, movies, and yes, even Santa, the Tooth Fairy, and the Easter Bunny. Our preschoolers knew these were all pretend. They are wonderful, entertaining, and magical—but they are imaginary. If you make pretend fun, we believe you rob nothing from these memories of childhood.

While imagination is a wonderful gift, kids need a strong sense of what is real. Real is everything God says in His Word, the Bible. Real is Mommy and Daddy's love for God, each other, and their children. Children should be taught that everything should be run through the grid of what is real and true: media, what friends say, what teachers teach, etc. When it comes to love, romance, and sexual activity, much of what our kids will be exposed to is fabricated by the entertainment industry. Having a track record of wisely telling the truth gives you credibility later on when your children need to decide what is true about their sexual lives.

Progressive Exposure

Ah, now this is where the rubber meets the road. How much of the truth about sex do we tell our kids—and more importantly, when do we tell them what? Children have a natural curiosity and a natural innocence. You have a natural desire for them to know the truth and a natural desire to protect them. You also have a balancing act between disclosing just the right amount of vital information to inform and protect them and keeping your own privacy about your love life and marriage. We ran a few questions through our minds as we discussed the topic of sex and how we'd communicate it to our children as they grew up. We asked questions of ourselves like:

- What do they need to know right now to keep them safe from mistruths?

- What do they need to *not* hear to keep their innocence?

- What can wait until later as the next layer of information?

- What can I share that will help them respect the sanctity, purity, and privacy of a married sexual relationship?

- What is the minimum I can share on this topic before I expose them to something they might not be ready to hear?

Instead of starting at birth and working forward, we started at their wedding day and worked backward, listing off what they needed to know and when they would need to know it. Here is a brief (non-exhaustive) list similar to the one we tallied when our oldest was a toddler:

Before marriage they will need to know: The basics on how sex organs work and the process their heart, mind, body, and soul would need to go through for a happy, healthy sexual encounter. If they are not ready to become parents as a couple, then they will need to know contraceptive options. They also will need the wisdom to have waited for the "I do" so their sexual baggage is minimal or perhaps nonexistent. They will need to know how to get reliable education and advice on sexually pleasing their mate. They will also need to be informed about adjustments and transitions to expect on the road ahead as a married couple.

Before college they will need to know: Street smarts to protect them from being in dangerous situations such as in a car with a drunk driver, at a party where drinking is happening, or alone where date rape could occur. Before launching from the umbrella of your home, a college student needs enough information to realize when they felt sexual attraction. Then they will need to know how to manage that attraction in order to live with integrity. They will also need information so they can "pre-decide" and defend decisions on crucial topics like premarital sex, the sacred aspect of marriage, gender identity, pro-life and abortion, and principles of dating in order to wisely select a lifelong marriage partner.

Before high school they will need to know: How to be aware of and manage their sexual feelings. They need a strong self-esteem to be able to say *no* to negative peer pressure. They should have ability to handle critical choices that might place them in compromising situations. It is imperative that they have the character and courage to defend their beliefs and values. They also need to know how to walk away from relationships that might be pulling them away from God's plan for their lives. They should have the ability to be the leaders of their peers, setting the example relating to adults and their friends in a way to build trust. They need people skills to help keep others around them honest, safe, and making better choices. They will need to be convinced of the negative consequences of sex outside of marriage and how to defend their beliefs. They need to be aware of the basic types of contraception options so they can defend their choice of abstinence and avoid the myth of safe sex. They need just enough information about how sexual organs work so they could not be fooled into experimenting with foreplay, oral sex, or other dangerous sexual behaviors.

Before junior high they will need to know: Much of this same information, but not in as much detail as they will be living a more supervised life. They will need enough information to defend their moral beliefs and values but not so much as to peak their curiosity into wanting to experiment. They will also need to know how to handle pressure not just from peers, but from any adult who might be seeking to defile, harm, "educate," or persuade them away from the values you have instilled. They will need enough street smarts to keep themselves safe. They will need to know how to handle any persecution of their values and how to recognize and defend themselves against sexual harassment or intimidation of any kind.

Before most of their classmates have begun to menstruate or have wet dreams: The average age for girls to begin their periods in the United States is 12, but girls as young as 8 can start menstruating. Sperm and ejaculation typically occur between the ages of 12 and 15, but could be as young as 10. So around age 8 might be a wise time to prepare both genders for the upcoming changes in their bodies (we will go over this in more detail in a future chapter). Your children need to be prepared *before* the changes start in their own bodies or in the bodies of their classmates. They need to understand the major changes they might notice in those of the opposite sex so they can be tactful, helpful, and good friends to those of both genders. They will also need to know enough about the act of sexual intercourse so that no one could take advantage of or mislead him or her. They will need a strong self-image to navigate all the body changes and social awkwardness that sometimes accompanies these changes.

Before entering school (typically at age 5): They need to know enough to protect themselves from predators. They also need a way to protect themselves from misinformation or peers who might come from homes where there are older siblings, uninvolved parents, or more exposure to unhealthy media messages. They need to know basic body parts that might come up in conversation and how to handle slang or inappropriate language or behavior. They also need to know how to speak up and step away from situations that make them feel uncomfortable. They need to know enough about how babies are made and how our bodies work so they understand the important transitions around them like weddings, pregnancy, and babies being born. They should be able to comprehend modesty and why it is important in society. They need the foundations of good moral choices like truthfulness, delayed gratification, wisdom, and obedience to God and parents.

By walking the path backward, we clearly saw there were at least six major talks or six "marker moments." These would be times when we deliberately set aside the space to talk, prepared necessary resources to clearly communicate, and saved the money to appropriately celebrate the child at these marker moments. We will walk you through these moments in more detail and give you resources, tools, and insights you will need to equip your child along their path to adult sexual health. We also know that much is communicated between the marker moments, so we will seek to fill in the blanks so that you can respond to a child's teachable moments and have answers ready when God might prompt you into a conversation or a child is inquisitive enough to ask a question.

Explanations

Our advice is to gather the tools and then get ready to use them at natural intervals, layer upon layer. When your child is very young, you'll need to be able to answer these questions:

- What is a boy/girl?
- How did I get here?

- Where do babies come from?
- What is sex? (or making love, or a term for intercourse you are comfortable with)

If you are feeling a little apprehensive, unsure, or anxious, you are in good company. Even Jim Burns, parenting expert, bestselling author, and host of *HomeWord* radio show felt that way in the beginning:

> When Cathy and I became parents, we had basically no clue about teaching healthy sexuality to our kids. When our first daughter, Christy, was about one, I vaguely remember helping her learn the names of body parts. We focused on the nose, ears, eyes, hands, feet, etc., but missed some pretty important private parts. By the time our next child, Rebecca, came along, we corrected the situation and taught her the proper terms for those body parts. And then at inopportune moments, like in a crowded store or in the middle of a church service, she would shout out that a particular body part itched! People would look at us like we had corrupted our child. To say the least, our sex-education "method" was trial-and-error at first. [2]

Name It

The first step is to help the child know about his or her body—all the parts! As Linda and Richard Eyre put it, "A healthy attitude about sex starts with how a child feels about his own body. At a very young age children become aware of their bodies and what they can do. In fact, studies have shown that over 80 percent of what we learn about our physical bodies is learned in the first eighteen months of life." [3]

We think it is best to use proper anatomical terms for body parts. Just as you play the game naming eyes, ears, and elbows, when a child points at private parts be sure he or she knows the accurate labels rather than referring to them with nicknames. Once our children were familiar with the names of sexual organs visible from the exterior, we generally summed this up as "your privates." This proved to be less stressful for a child to use in public. For example, "I fell and my privates hurt," or "The ball hit my privates."

Anatomy 101

Let's go over what parts you should know. From there, it will be up to you to decide when to teach the anatomy to your child. We have listed these as which parts you can see on the outside and which ones the child can't see. We suggest starting with the exterior now and moving on to the interior parts (and their functions) as your child matures and you continue this dialogue.

Girls

What you can see:	*What you can't see:*
Outer labia	Ovaries
Inner labia	Fallopian tubes
Vulva (clitoris, vagina)	Uterus
Urethra opening	Cervix

Boys

What you can see:	*What you can't see:*
Penis head	Urethra
Penis shaft	Prostate
Urethra opening	Glands that channel sperm down penis
Scrotum	
Foreskin (if uncircumcised)	

A simple and natural way to begin the process of enlightening your child to his or her basic body parts is to play the "What's this?" game at bath time. Just as you would name a nose or elbow, name the exterior parts. You can either wait for them to ask the name of the body part or set a time to purposefully teach a child (maybe if he or she has an older sibling who might use the terms, or so they know the terms before entering preschool). Remember the overall rule: *Let them hear God's truth and good information from you before they hear it from anyone else*. You as the parent are the best sex ed teacher for your child because you care most about their life and the outcome of all the instruction and teaching you give.

Inquisitive Learners

Some misconceptions about where babies come from are a bit entertaining:

> One little girl thought babies were made by magic. Some children believe the stork brings babies. Others think we grow like plants or hatch eggs. One little boy was told that the father plants a seed inside the mom and a baby grows. He wondered whether they used a shovel![4]

In the early years sexual education comes in baby steps. Your child probably won't stop asking questions. Just about every sentence they utter starts with *why, how,* or *what.* And sooner or later, this curiosity will spread to questions about the body.

A few questions to be ready for might include:

- What's this? Why do I have one?
- Will my penis fall off?
- Why is Daddy's bigger?
- Why do boys stand up and girls sit down to go potty?
- How can you tell if a baby is a boy or a girl?
- Why are you so fat? (to a pregnant mom)
- Why don't I have a penis?
- Why are Mommy's breasts big and mine are small?

Ask First

For this chapter, the overall umbrella question is, "Where did I come from?" It often lands in your lap when a child is three or four.

Before answering, pause and consider what Dr. J. Thomas Fitch of the Medical Institute for Sexual Health suggests:

> With this question, your child could be asking any number of things. You can assess what she really wants to know by asking, "What do you mean?" Her response to the question will let you know if she's inquiring about birth or whether she's asking a theological question ("Who made me?") or a geographic question ("Did I come from Alabama like Johnny?"). In fact, the response "What do you mean?" is one of the best tools you have to teach your child of any age about sex. [5]

Keep It Simple!

Usually your child's inquisitive nature will prepare you for the need to get some answers ready. Sexual Educator Laurie Langford says,

> Sometimes a three, four, or five-year-old will ask questions about her body, such as, "Why don't I have a penis?" Just answer your child's questions honestly and nonchalantly. You could say, "Because you are a girl, and girls have vaginas. Only boys have penises." [6]

Some type of basic answer should be prepared in your mind, but don't feel compelled to give all the details too early. Linda and Richard Eyre recommend this approach to talking to your children about sex:

> If a five-year-old says, "Where do babies come from?" say, "Sometimes when a mommy and a daddy love each other, it helps make a baby." If he says, "But how?" say, "It's like a miracle, a wonderful, unbelievable magic. When you're eight, we'll tell you about it."...Then change the subject unless you detect that the child is troubled or worried or has heard something that is causing him to persist. If this is the case, probe. Find out what he has heard or what has happened. If it's just a word or a term he's heard that he doesn't understand, give your best explanation...You may

want to say, "Some people joke around or say weird things about stuff you don't understand. But don't worry, we'll tell you all about it when you're eight. And believe me, it is wonderful and way cool!"[7]

At the age of eight, children can handle more abstract thinking and their social lives begin to change with the onset of menses right around the corner for some girls. At this early stage, however, kids still think in concrete terms and do best with simple explanations. Before you answer a question, keep your audience in mind. "You're talking to children who can't remember which shoe goes on which foot without regular reminders."[8]

Answers to Have Ready

Your family has its own comfort level and maturity level when it comes to these personal conversations, but it's always helpful to see how different parents approach the issue. This is an example of how we handled those early question-and-answer sessions in preschool and early elementary school (when our children were toddlers up to about age seven). Our early conversations with our oldest, Brock, while expecting our second baby, were more like a bouncing ball. We might bounce a ball once or twice then put it in a pocket. Later we would get it out and bounce it again.

Bounce 1

Mom and Dad: Brock, we have some happy news!

Brock: What?

Mom and Dad: You are going to have a little brother or sister!

Brock: I am? Which one, a brother or a sister?

Mom and Dad: We don't know yet. We will have to wait until the baby is born and we will find out together. (We liked having the surprise.)

Brock: When will the baby be born?

Mom and Dad: In about six more months.

Brock: Okay. Can I go play now?

Bounce 2

Mom and Dad: Brock, we have a special book to read to you. (We bought a picture book with real photos of a baby in the uterus.) Mommy and Daddy love each other very much, so we hugged and cuddled a very special way. It is called sex, and God designed it for married couples. When mommies and daddies love each other this way, a little sperm, or little seed, is planted inside the mommy's womb. A womb is a special place inside Mommy under her tummy about right here. (I placed Brock's hand on my tummy.) Inside, the seed and one of Mommy's special tiny eggs linked together and made a new tiny baby. That baby is growing and growing, like we saw in the picture book. Mommy's belly will get bigger and bigger and then one day my womb will squeeze really, really tight. That is called a contraction, and Daddy will drive me to the hospital and Grandma will stay here with you. At the hospital the doctor will help your little brother or sister be born and you can come to the hospital and visit me and the new baby. So Brock, tell me, how is a baby created?

Brock: God puts a baby inside Mommy's tummy. Then it gets big and then you go to the hospital and the baby gets born.

Mom: That's right.

Bounce 3

Brock: Mommy, can we take the baby out and play?

Mom: Not yet. The baby isn't big enough yet. The baby needs to grow for a little longer in Mommy's tummy.

Brock: Aaaahhh! I want to play with my brother or sister. Can we play with the baby tomorrow?

Mom: Come let me show you on the calendar how many more days. Let's count them together. (Some families make a paper chain and take one link off each day.)

Brock : 152 days! That is a long time!

Bounce 4

Brock: How will the baby get out of your tummy?

Mom: Well, God made it so Mommy has a special opening between her legs called a vagina and right now it is closed tight. When the baby is ready, God makes that opening get bigger and bigger so it is just the right size for a baby to slide out into the doctor's hands. Then the doctor gives the baby to Mommy and Daddy. But sometimes the baby might get a little stuck or a mommy's body might not work just right, and that's why the doctor is there. Like when you were born, the cord that attaches the baby to the mommy got all wrapped around your body and the doctor had to cut a little slit in my tummy, like a zipper. He took you out that way because he had to unwrap that cord. Want to see Mommy's zipper? (I showed my scar on my lower abdomen.)

Brock: Will this baby come out through that zipper?

Mom: Maybe. We will see how Mommy's body acts this time and what happens with the cord. I am so thankful that the doctor was there to help deliver you. I am so happy you are my little boy.

Brock: Me too. I love you, Mommy.

Mom: I love you, Brock.

Bounce 5

One day, walking from children's church with an older woman friend, Brock was holding my hand.

Friend: Brock, are you excited to have a new baby brother or sister?

Brock: Yep!

Friend: Do you want a brother or a sister?

Brock: I want a baby!

Friend: How did you explain the birds and the bees to Brock? What did you tell him about how the baby was made?

Brock: Mommy and Daddy had sex! (My friend blushed.)

Mom: That's right, Brock. And what is sex?

Brock: When a mommy and a daddy cuddle and love a special way to make a baby.

Mom: That's right. And who is supposed to have sex?

Brock: You are supposed to be married. It is for mommies and daddies so we can make a family. (My friend relaxed a bit when she heard this!)

Friend: He seems to know the right answers.

Mom to friend: We wanted to tell him God's plan before others confused him by doing things out of order.

Friend: I wish I had thought of that for my kids.

Mom to friend: Today's world demands we be proactive and teach God's design, God's definitions, and God's plan first before the world gets a shot at our precious kids.

Friend: Amen. So true.

Later, at home

Mom to Brock: Honey, it might be good if you didn't use the word *sex* when you're talking to other kids. Every family has their own way of talking about babies and their own time to talk about it, so let's let the mommies and daddies explain it to their own kids, okay?

Brock: You mean like Santa and Christmas?

Mom: Well, a little. Yes, each family has ways to talk about happy surprises like babies. So if one of your friends asks how this baby got into my belly, let's say to them, "You should ask your mommy and daddy. They are smart and they can tell you." Okay? So if one of your friends asks how this baby got in my tummy, what will you say?

Brock: You should ask your mommy or daddy because they will know!

Mom: Good job, Brock. That's right!

Bounce 6

Brock: What are you doing?

Mom: It is called nursing. The baby is drinking milk from my breasts. Remember how we went to the class at the hospital and they showed you how babies eat from the mommy's breast?

Brock: (lifting a Cabbage Patch doll under his shirt) Look, my baby is nursing!

Mom: That is a nice thought, and I'm glad you love your baby like I love your brother and I love you. Milk helps babies grow big and strong. But only mommies are made so that milk comes from their breasts. Boys and daddies don't have that ability. They can do other really cool stuff, but breastfeeding isn't one of them. Can you tell me all the cool things boys and daddies can do for a baby? (Then we helped him list things like carry the baby, change the baby, rock the baby, work hard for the money to pay for the house and a bed for the baby, etc.)

Another way to tactfully explain sexuality to a child is found in Carolyn Nystrom's book *Before I Was Born:*

> Friends bring gifts to a wedding. God has a special gift for new husbands and wives too. It is called sex. God's rules say that only people who are married to each other should have sex. It is God's way of making families strong.
>
> Because the man and woman are married, their bodies belong to each other. They enjoy holding each other close. When a husband and a wife lie close together, he can fit his penis into her vagina. His semen flows inside her and their bodies feel good all over. Husbands and wives want to be alone during sex so they can think only of each other.
>
> This is the way babies are made. A husband can't make a baby by himself. A wife can't make a baby by herself. But God made their bodies so they fit perfectly together. And together they can make a baby.[9]

Parent to Parent

You all have family and friends visit, so you will need to make a decision on how your child will dress (or not) when company is around.

Toddlers and preschoolers are all about being "naked and not ashamed." So what are some of the issues that might need to be "covered" as a child moves from freely wearing his or her birthday suit to wanting privacy and needing modesty to function appropriately in society? Thomas Fitch explains:

> Typically toddlers and younger preschoolers have no sense of embarrassment about their bodies and love to run around the house naked. This is a natural desire and doesn't mean our child will vacation at nudist camps in the future. Between the ages of four and six, most kids develop a sense of privacy and limit the time they spend naked.
>
> There are certain situations, however, such as when guests who might be…bothered by the nakedness are in your home, when your child shouldn't run around naked. Simply explain to her that being naked in public or when guests are in the house isn't good manners. Unless you are uncomfortable with your child's nudity, allow her to outgrow this phase on her own.[10]

Questions for Your Heart

Being caught in the act is one of the most awkward moments for the parents of a preschooler. Doors are often left ajar so a baby or toddler can be heard if they wake up at night. This precaution can, however, lead to some interesting surprises!

One night we were enjoying each other sexually when one of our preschool sons threw the door open and said sleepily, "Mommy, Daddy, I had a bad dream."

Not wanting to be a part of the dream, we simply said, "Honey, shut the door and wait outside. Mommy and Daddy will be right there to help you."

Tossing on our robes (keep these close while raising little ones!), we scooped him up. Once we calmed his nightmare fears, he asked, "Daddy and Mommy, what were you doing? You made funny noises."

We looked at each other and because we had talked *before* this episode about what we might say if something like this happened, we said, "Yes, Mommy and Daddy do make funny noises sometimes when we kiss and hug and love each other. But they are happy noises and someday when you get married you will love your wife as much as I love Daddy. Won't that be wonderful? Because then you can have a little boy and you can love him as much as we love you!"

He gave us a big hug and kiss, and said, "I love you, Mommy. I love you, Daddy." Then there was a pause. "But what if I have a girl?"

"Then you will love her just as much!" we replied confidently.

"Are you sure? She's a girl!"

"We are sure because God makes everyone in an amazing way."

Take out your journal, interview your spouse, and make some notes about what you think the appropriate response would be if you were "surprised" by your child (if they walk in on an intimate moment or while you are changing clothes or using the bathroom). It is easier to reply in a calm manner and instruct rather than lose your cool if you have thought about these things ahead of time.

Can You Give Me a Strong Foundation?

> But the wisdom that comes from heaven is first of all pure;
> then peace-loving, considerate, submissive, full of
> mercy and good fruit, impartial and sincere.
>
> James 3:17

We had the privilege of building our home in the suburbs of San Diego. If you know anything about earthquakes and fault lines, you know the great San Andreas Fault runs the length of California. To meet code, our home was built to withstand at least a 6.0 earthquake. Bill went above and beyond, putting steel rebar into the concrete foundation. His extra time and effort was worth it. Since we built the home there have been at least three sizeable quakes that should have knocked it to the ground. Other homes were damaged, but not ours! We are rock solid!

In a state that has more than 500 earthquakes each year that are strong enough to be felt, it is vital to have a strong foundation and be prepared.[1] The good news is, just as a building can be retrofitted to strengthen it against a quake, you can go back and retrofit your family's foundations. If your children are still young, you can create a plan to lay a strong foundation from the very beginning. So what is a strong foundation, and how do you lay one?

Secure Footings

When we built our home, Bill dug deep to place steel rebar footings in so the foundation wouldn't slide and crack. In the same way, if we help our kids appreciate the value of digging deep into God's Word, their lives are less likely to slide from the securely centered and healthy foundation you are laying for their lives.

Truth Is Secure

There are many reasons we believe that the Bible is true. Let's look at just three of them.

First, *God's Word proclaims it.* John 17:17 says, "Sanctify them by the truth; your word is truth." And this truth is eternal. First Peter 1:24-25 says, "All people are like grass, and all their glory is like the flowers of the field; the grass withers and the flowers fall, but the word of the Lord endures forever." God Himself has proclaimed that the Bible is true!

Second, *history and science have caught up to the truth of the Bible.* For much of early history, people thought the earth was flat. In Isaiah 40:22 the prophet boldly proclaims, "He sits enthroned above the circle of the earth." He wrote this before the concept of a spherical earth was first theorized by the ancient Greeks—and *well* before the idea was finally proven!

This is just one simple example of science and history catching up to the truth of God's Word. There are ample examples, and exploring more of this kind of truth with your child will also create a secure environment. We enjoyed many children's resources from the Creation Studies Institute, the homeschooling world, and Christian bookstores.

Finally, *our lives echo the truth of the Word.* God declares certain things will happen when you come into a personal relationship with Jesus. You will be able to understand the Word, live out the fruit of God's Spirit, and turn from darkness into God's wonderful light. Our personal stories and yours, once you begin a relationship with Jesus, reflect the power of the truth of God's Word. Job 19:25 declares, "I know that my redeemer lives, and that in the end he will stand on the earth." Revelation 12:11 gives an example of victory over Satan; "They triumphed over him by the blood of the Lamb and by the word of their testimony." Believers throughout the centuries have been so convinced of the truth that they have risked their lives to spread it far and wide.

As you interact with your child, remark on it when you see God being faithful to His Word. While teaching at a family conference in Cannon Beach, we met an amazing military family that had home-schooled all of their eight children. Most of the children were grown and were leaders in their careers, communities, and churches. As I interacted with the mom, she would say, "Wow! God did that!" After a few days of receiving her exuberant reply back while conversing, I asked her about her personal tagline of "God did that!" She said she had been saying it to her children all day, every day, for most of their lives as she saw God intervene or be faithful to His promises. It is no wonder all of her kids are equally excited about life, leadership, and following a God who "did that!"

When a child sees God is real and His truth reigns, that child will more easily obey and honor that truth. Stan and Brenna Jones emphasize the connection sex education has with an accurate view of God and God's truth:

> Here is our vision: that children grow up with godly, age-appropriate discussion and teaching about sexuality as a regular part of their relationships with their parents. Why? Because parents are God's agents for shaping the sexual characters of their children. And we believe that both parents and children can trust God's wisdom about sexuality throughout their lives, because that wisdom is given for their good.[2]

Truth Is Two-Sided

To make wise choices in your personal life, one must see truth as a two-way street. God gives truth, and that truth must be seen as ultimate truth, a truth that trumps all other opinions. And because God's truth is preeminent, it ranks higher than the media, educational systems, or family patterns. Once a person views God's Word as the final say, it is easier to choose to obey and live in harmony with it.

We played an ongoing game with our kids over the years we called, "Does It Match?" You might be familiar with the card game where you lay cards facedown on the floor or a table and flip them over one at a time, trying to make pairs from memory. We adapted this concept with our kids so that cartoons, TV shows, movies, or people's life choices would all be filtered through the truth of God's Word. We would ask, "Does this match up?"

Let me give a few examples of what this might look like in everyday life at various ages and stages of development:

Preschool through early elementary: While watching a cartoon, if something didn't match up to God's Word the TV went off and we used it as a learning time. For example, one day while our sons were watching "Teenage Mutant Ninja Turtles" the turtles began chanting a mantra common in Eastern mystic religions. I (Pam) shut the TV off, opened up the Bible to the 10 Commandments, and read about God's command to have "no other gods." I then flipped through a few Old Testament Bible stories that gave examples of what happened to people who didn't give God all their worship.

After I read the negative stories and explained what God took away for disobedience, I would find stories showing God's blessings for obedience. Then we would act those stories out or come up with a game to illustrate the lesson. I was a pretty cool mom in the eyes of the three sons as I helped make swords and shields so they could defeat the armies of the Philistines. (It's amazing what a little duct tape and a rolled-up newspaper can become in the hands of a mighty warrior for God!)

To pull this off, you as a parent have to make two commitments. First, you can't use the TV as a babysitter. You have to at least be within earshot and tuned in enough to hear the plotline and vocabulary of what's playing. Second, you have to know what is in God's Word yourself so you can lead the matching game.

Later elementary through early junior high: After our children could read fast enough to read what was printed on a TV screen (usually around second grade), we rewarded self-initiated discernment. We had a "Discernment jar" for each child, and any good decision could result in a marble being dropped into his jar. Good behavior, good actions toward another, and good discretion in media choices could all garner a marble. A quick example might be when the boys were watching a pre-approved television channel and spotted something that went against God's Word (a magic spell, for example). If they shut off the TV and came to us so we could go back and watch with them and talk about what they saw, they would get a marble in the jar. We discovered even Disney and some of the family channels began to slip into some non-biblical choices. Sometimes they would show engaged couples sleeping together (even if sex was not shown) or two men or two women raising a child. Sometimes a few swear words slipped through.

When the jar was full, they could go to the local Christian bookstore and buy a new book, movie, or CD. We liked to reward good discernment with tools to promote more good discernment! In junior high, we expanded the shopping options to include favorite sporting goods stores as well.

Junior high on up: At this point we kicked the *Teen Media Contract* into place. (We'll discuss this in detail in a future chapter.) As parents, we wanted to roll the ball into their court—although we retained veto power if they completely missed the mark! With the contract came the privilege and responsibility of buying their own media with their own money. We did offer some ways to earn more money. If they read a book (either a Christian book or one from a list of classics) and discussed it with us, we would give them a gift card to buy another book (or movie or CD) from the Christian bookstore.

Decisions That Protect

Discernment doesn't just happen. Kids will naturally slide to the lowest common denominator. God tells us we must teach discernment. In Psalm 119:66 (NASB) the psalmist writes, "Teach me good discernment and knowledge, for I believe in your commandments." And in Proverbs 1:4-5 (NASB) we learn, "To give prudence to the naïve, to the youth knowledge and discretion, a wise man will hear and increase in learning, and a man of understanding will acquire wise counsel."

So we are to pray for and practice good discernment and knowledge (knowledge is what you learn; discernment is how you apply it). Invite your child to grow into more and more responsibility in gaining the wisdom he or she needs. Teach your son or daughter to prioritize, pray for, and pursue discernment and wisdom, much like Solomon asked for in 1 Kings 3:9-14:

> "So give your servant a discerning heart to govern your people and to distinguish between right and wrong. For who is able to govern this great people of yours?" The Lord was pleased that Solomon had asked for this. So God said to him, "Since you have asked for this and not for long life or wealth for yourself, nor have asked for the death of your enemies but for discernment in administering justice, I will do what you have asked. I will give you a wise and discerning heart, so that there will never have been anyone like you, nor will there ever be. Moreover, I will give you what you have not asked for—both wealth and honor—so that in your lifetime you will have no equal among kings. And if you walk in obedience to me and keep my decrees and commands as David your father did, I will give you a long life."

Seek the Answers to Foundational Questions

In these early years, you need your own pursuit of wisdom. You will have your own list of questions that might come up, but here are some common ones with answers so you can be prepared:

When is it okay to change a child's clothing in public?

Diaper changing sets a reliable pattern in place. Because of the smell of diaper changing, most parents look for a place away from the crowd to change a diaper. A similar choice is wise as you move into the potty training stage. When your child is a toddler, train both yourself and your child to always look for a private place (a car, bathroom, etc.) for the quick change. When the child is about three, listen to him or her for clues about being uncomfortable changing in public.

Who should a child bathe or shower with?

A simple way to know things need to change in having the kids in the tub together is if one child becomes uncomfortable or asks too many questions. Don't allow too much touching or "playing doctor." To save time, some parents will take a small child into the tub or shower with them. If you are the opposite gender, stop this practice when the child becomes aware of your gender and comments on it, or if any negative or uncomfortable feelings arise in you. If you are never comfortable, then never do it. Even if you are the same gender, if the child begins asking uncomfortable questions or touching in an inquisitive way, or if you are feeling uncomfortable in any way, then it is time to allow the child to bathe more independently.

What if my child sees me naked?

Dr. Thomas Fitch suggests:

> Young children are often present with parents of either sex as they dress. This is natural. As your child gets older and more verbal, he may ask questions about the shape and look of your body…Again, such questions are normal and healthy. This provides another teachable moment for the discussion of anatomy. Privacy should become more the rule when the parent or child is uncomfortable with exposure. In general, by the time your child is four or five, you shouldn't be naked intentionally around him. Accidental exposure now and then isn't a problem during the pre-school and early elementary years.[3]

Parents shouldn't be freaked out by a child's willing nudity, yet we parents should also be respectful of the proper time, place, and amount of nudity we condone. Too much nudity too early can lead to early desensitization of a child's mind, while overreaction implants a negative memory toward their bodies or nakedness in general, which could be a problem if it crops up later as an adult. Stan and Brenna Jones lay a simple principle in place: "We would recommend that parents not obsessively guard against seeing family members naked [at this preschool stage], but also that nudity not be flaunted in the family."[4]

What if I discover my child playing doctor?

Dr. Steven Atkins gives a commonsense answer to the predicament of discovering children playing doctor:

> It can be kind of a shock to walk in on your preschooler and her friend to discover they both have their pants down and one is giving the other a shot on the bottom. While it is not unusual for kids this age to be curious about each other's bodies, and to want to learn about them, they need to know that touching other people's private parts is off limits. If you discover [children] playing doctor don't scold them and make them feel ashamed of themselves. Instead, very calmly tell them to pull their pants up and let them know that everyone has private parts that aren't for touching. Then redirect their play. Later on bring it up with your child and ask her if she has any questions about her body and answer those questions honestly and matter-of-factly. You should also talk with the other child's parents about what happened so they are aware of how you handled the situation. This is a good opportunity to talk with the other parents about how they would handle a similar situation. It's always useful to know where other parents stand on things, and whether or not you agree with the way they'd approach various issues. After all, you are entrusting your child to their care when she is at their house.[5]

As a parent, be aware that there is a difference between "playing doctor" with another child approximately your child's same age, which can be a simple display of curiosity, and molestation that can be inflicted by an older child upon a younger one (often because that child has been sexually abused by another person).

What if I discover my preschooler touching himself?

Preschoolers spend a lot of time touching themselves, but at this early stage it is not masturbation but rather a way of self-soothing. However, the behavior should be handled, not ignored. If ignored, it can grow into an issue. If you observe this behavior, say something like, "It feels good to have the water run over your penis, doesn't it? (Or to touch your privates.) That is because God made our bodies to feel good. But that part of your body is private. It is special. It is special because when we get married someday, we can love each other in a special way. So, honey, this touching is not for you to do right now." Then distract the child with another activity. If the behavior is constant (many times every day for months, much more than their friends the same age), consult a pediatrician or therapist.

What if a friend or child in our home uses words we do not approve of?

If a child (yours or a friend's) brings home a slang word, assume they are confused and set the record straight by simply explaining, "We don't use that word in our home or family. Some people use that word to mean [explain the definition in a way that preserves as much of your child's innocence as possible]. So from now on we won't use that word, okay?"

We then took the next step and asked where our child heard the word. We would then pray about what we would do. Some steps might include talking to that child's parents and carefully monitoring the time our children spent in his or her company.

How long can my child use opposite gender's bathroom?

This one used to be easier in generations past when life was safer. A good rule of thumb used to be that if a child could read the words on a public restroom door, it was time for them to use the bathroom assigned to their gender. However, extra precaution should be taken on behalf of the child even if it makes a few adults a little uncomfortable.

When our sons were growing up, a boy in junior high was assaulted and stabbed to death in a public restroom at the same beach our family always visited. Until that moment, everyone felt safe. The bathrooms were nice and clean and there were usually plenty of good families and moral people around. However, when this young man didn't return, the aunt who was nearby went into the bathroom and found her nephew dead from stab wounds. Eventually, a known pedophile living nearby was arrested. When this happened, our oldest son was also in junior high.

We had always tried to send our sons either with their dad, a friend, or another brother to any public bathroom. Going in pairs was mandatory. If I was alone with a son and he was over the age of six, I would allow him to use the men's bathroom but I would stand outside the door. We had an agreed-upon time limit. If my son didn't come out in that time, I would first ask a man exiting to go back in and ask, "Is there a boy in here whose mom is Pam?" (I didn't want strange men to know my son's name.) If no man exited, I would prop the door open and simply say, "Is anyone in there?" Typically my son would shout out and I could verbally check on his safety.

Having your mom stand outside the public bathroom might be a bit embarrassing, but if you play it cool and simply act nonchalant, it doesn't need to be something that embarrasses him or threatens his masculinity. And at *least* equal precaution should be taken with a daughter. Trust your gut. In some settings, like at church or your kid's school, you might be able to allow kids to fly solo to use the facilities, but again, if in doubt, don't risk it.

Keeping the Foundation from Fracture

In a world that is more and more sexually saturated, with societal restraints and morality being worn away, our kids are more at risk than ever of being victimized by sexual predators. A third of all girls and a quarter of all boys will be sexually molested between the ages of four and nine. [6] The pain reverberates: "Eighty percent of the people I work with who struggle with sexual sin were sexually abused as children," notes Mark Laaser. [7] This is a parent's worst nightmare, so let's discuss how to protect the kids.

Only seven percent of children are molested by strangers. That means ninety-three percent of children who are molested are abused by people they know and trust. The likelihood of sexual abuse doubles in a blended family. Stepbrothers and stepfathers are the most likely per- petrators. Children who are at higher risk include those with a mother with a negative view of sexuality, those who are isolated from friends and have a poor relationship with their parents, those living in poverty, and those whose parents are poorly educated.[8] Also at risk are children who don't have a strong male role model at home, those who are shy or disabled, and those who are quite naïve (lacking street smarts or that "something is wrong here" gut feeling).

We hate to have to prepare you with this information, but you should know the tell-tale signs of concern that should alert you that sexual abuse may have occurred. Your child might experience behav- ioral problems or be showing signs of physical pain or changes (includ- ing vaginal or rectal bleeding, pain, itching, swollen genitals, discharge or infections). Your child's behavior might become suddenly sexual- ized by things like compulsive genital touching, overt sexual actions or comments, or seductive or inappropriate behaviors or comments. You might also see more subtle emotional changes like sleep problems, depression, withdrawal, a lower sense of self-worth, fear, anger, or anx- iety if you leave his or her presence, and a sudden tendency to keep secrets.

Profile of a Pedophile

Most molesters are male and typically over 30. Most sexual abuse is by a family member. The most frequent type (but least talked about) is an older brother molesting a younger sister; it is five times more com- mon than the most publicized type—a father molesting a daughter. The majority of molesters are single. If married, their union usually lacks intimacy. The abuser is often also a past victim of child molesta- tion himself.

If you are new to a friendship, look for these warning signs:

- He has gaps in his employment or personal history (which might reflect jail time or moving to avoid being caught).

- He is often fascinated with children and prefers children's activities.

- He will often refer to children in pure or angelic terms, using descriptions like *innocent, heavenly, divine, pure,* and other words that describe children but seem exaggerated.

- He has hobbies that are childlike, such as collecting popular expensive toys, keeping reptiles or exotic pets, or building plane and car models.

- He has few friends his age.

Pedophiles often target children of a specific age. Some prefer younger children, some older. He often seeks out children of the same age he was when he was victimized. Many pedophiles seek out children close to puberty who are sexually inexperienced, but curious about sex. Often his environment will be decorated in childlike decor and will appeal to the age and sex of the child he is trying to entice.

The pedophile will often be employed or volunteer in a position that involves daily contact with children. This will often be in a supervisory capacity such as sports coaching, unsupervised tutoring, or a position where he has the opportunity to spend unsupervised time with a child. He might chaperone camping or overnight trips; frequent video arcades, playgrounds, or shopping malls; offer babysitting services; participate in internet gaming with children; join social networking websites; and even become a foster parent and betray those who most need to be protected. They may frequent children's events even if they have no children or grandchildren.

The pedophile often seeks out those who come from troubled or underprivileged homes. He then showers them with attention and gifts, enticing them with trips to desirable places like amusement parks, zoos, concerts, or the beach.

Pedophiles are masters of manipulation. They first become a child's friend, building up his or her self-esteem. They may refer to the child as *special* or *mature,* appealing to their need to be heard and understood and then enticing them with adult-type activities that are often sexual in content, such as viewing X-rated movies or pictures. They offer them alcohol or drugs to hamper their ability to resist activities or recall events that occurred.

Many times pedophiles will develop a close relationship with a single parent in order to get close to their children. Once inside the home, they have many opportunities to manipulate the children using guilt, fear, and love to confuse them. If the child's parent works outside the home, the pedophile has all the time he wants to abuse the child.

Pedophiles stalk their targets and will patiently work to develop relationships with them. It is not uncommon for them to be developing a long list of potential victims at any one time. One factor that works against the pedophile is that eventually the children will grow up and recall the events that occurred. Often pedophiles are not brought to justice until such time occurs and victims are angered by being victimized and want to protect other children from the same consequences. [9]

Sex offenders can be tough to spot on the surface as some are married and hardworking, employed within a wide range of occupations. They are usually well-liked and respected community members, and may even be well-educated and regular churchgoers. However, a more sure sign is that they relate better to children than to adults.

Answers to Have Ready

Create a **S.A.F.E.** place to grow up by checking a child's...

Skills to Speak Up

Teach your child that their body is private. They own their body and all rights to it. Teach your child as early as possible to close the door or go into a private room or bathroom to change his or her clothes. In addition, give your child the power to speak up and teach them that...

- It is never okay for anyone to touch your private parts (except a parent or doctor to protect your health).

- It is never okay for anyone to ask you to touch their private parts.

- It is never okay for anyone to ask to see you naked or ask you to see them naked.

- It is never okay for anyone to ask you to be sexual with someone else while they watch.[10]

- Don't explain—just go! Leave the person and the place.

- If you can't leave, yell for help!

- If they threaten you or your family, they are liars and weak. Go and tell!

- If they say it's your fault, don't believe them. Go and tell!

- If they promise gifts or money, it is not worth it. Go and tell!

- Tell your mom, your dad, your teachers, your pastor, or the police. Tell it until someone does something to stop it.

Tell your child that *No means no!* Reinforce this when your child is playing at home, even just roughhousing with you or siblings. If they say, "Stop!" abide by their wishes. Compliment your child when they give an opinion, speak up, correct others, or show leadership. Confident, courageous, assertive kids are harder targets for pedophiles.

Give your kids permission to tell you anything sexual in nature without worrying that you'll overreact. Satan's greatest tool is darkness, so when you shine the light by talking about this or any sexual topic, it is like taking a flashlight to a cockroach—they run for cover. If your child feels free to talk with you about his or her feelings about a friend, a family member, or a babysitter, you have a better chance of protecting them.

Adult Involvement

Are any adults showing uninvited attention toward your child? Do any adults or older teens show behaviors that make you or your child uneasy? In a church, school, or community setting have the adults been properly vetted to spot anyone who might have a background with sexual violations?

Trust your instincts! If you are in God's Word, praying, and doing your due diligence, you should trust your instincts as a parent to protect and equip your child to live in this broken world. If a girl feels uncomfortable with another adult touching even an acceptable area of the body, respect her instincts and allow them to guide your response. If a boy becomes shy or uncomfortable around a peer, older child, or adult, remove him from the situation while you gather more information. Give your son or daughter encouragement to always talk to you anytime someone makes him or her feel uncomfortable.

Friendship Circle

Do any of your child's friends have parents going through a family trauma (divorce, domestic violence, etc.)? Do any of your child's playmates have parents or older siblings with addictions to drugs, alcohol, or other behavior-altering substances? Do you know if any of your child's friends' siblings are sexually active or have been molested themselves?

If your child tells you about a playmate who is watching media you are uncomfortable with, if their playmates' parents are experiencing marital problems, or if they have much older siblings who seem to show overt and unusual amounts of attention to your child, put some space in the relationship. If you doubt the attentiveness of the parent of one of your child's playmates or if your child communicates neglect (saying that the parent is distracted or unavailable when your child is visiting), don't allow your child to visit their home alone. If you know a child has been sexually molested, make sure their interactions with your child are supervised at church, school, or in your home. It is just better to be safe than sorry.

Environment and Atmosphere

Are your yard and home difficult to access or walk into undetected? Do you have play spaces within the home in close proximity to the busy high traffic areas where adults can easily oversee children playing? Have you gone to a sex offender registry website to discover which homes in your neighborhood might have a convicted (but released) sexual offender living there?

If your child attends a church, community or school-sponsored class, are there at least two adults in the room, and are there windows and open doors to raise the adults' accountability?

If a child goes to others' homes, do you know the backgrounds of the adults and older siblings who live there? Do those parents give sufficient attention to children playing? Do you know and agree with the songs, TV, movies, or internet use of the homes that your child visits? Early sexual exposure can lower natural resistance toward sexual exploration or sexual games predators sometimes use.

One last note: If you discover that a friend, family member, or neighbor has a history of a sexual offense, ask this person for a meeting and simply explain that you have discovered some information that is troubling your heart. State what the information is, and then ask him to explain his story. Thank him and tell him you will be confirming his story before you discuss any future interactions between him and your family. By asking for their story and confirming it with a second source, you might discover an error in judgment of a young adult (perhaps sexual assault charges) filed by the zealous parent of a girl who had remorse over her premarital sex but didn't want to own up to being a willing partner. In many places around the world, little or no differentiation is made between violent serial sexual offenders and an 18-year-old youth whose teenage girlfriend complied with his sexual advances.

Consult a counselor, police officer, or other professional who can explain to you the relapse rate of various offenders. For example, pedophiles who are repeat offenders will likely reoffend, while a middle schooler or high schooler who is in treatment might be safe for your family to be around (in a very structured setting with consistent adult oversight). A teen who had a one-time sexual offense but came to Christ and has years of a clean record could be safe to interact with if your families are very close, although a clear plan would need to be in place for any family gathering. Always err on the side of the child's safety.

Parent to Parent

When talking with another parent at this stage, it will likely be to negotiate childcare and discuss privacy rules in the home where your child will visit or be cared for. Explain your comfort level in the vital areas and simply ask them if they are willing to accommodate you. Here are a few common examples:

"At our home, since we just have boys, the kids all take a bath together. There might be questions if the kids bathe with your girls. We would prefer not to have to put you in a place to have to be asked those kinds of questions, so would you mind if the boys bathed separately?"

"We just explained how this baby got inside mommy's tummy. We told Sarah that every family explains things differently and at different times, so if she happens to bring anything up, would you mind just telling her something like, 'Let's talk about something else right now and you can save that special conversation for your mom and dad.' Are you okay helping us push pause on her questions so we can deal with them later?"

Simply treat others as you would have them treat you and most of your parent-to-parent discussions should go smoothly. Sometimes these conversations turn into mentoring moments as some moms and dads might ask you how you handle some of these more sensitive topics. This is a wonderful time to dialogue about your values and beliefs. Be sure to not preach or lecture, but simply share, "What we believe is…" or "What we think God wants us to do is…" Explain your point of view and allow them time to process the information.

Answers for Your Heart

For you to gain the ability to lead your child in God's truth, you need to have a growing relationship with God in His Word. To grow, you must PLANT God's Word into your life consistently:

Probe: Ask questions, then go to mentors, Logos Bible Software, commentaries, or a study Bible for answers.

Listen: Hearing other people teach the Bible and relate how it is affecting their lives encourages growth in all of us.

Acquaint yourself: There is no substitute for reading God's Word consistently. Get a One-Year Bible or download a reading plan from a trusted ministry and try to read the Bible cover to cover.

Nail it down: Memorizing specific verses makes them readily accessible so they are ready when you or your kids need them most.

Think it over: Apply the Word with questions like, "How do I live this out? And how does this apply to my life?"

Truth is your ally. When you lay out God's truth of what is right and wrong in the area of sexuality, piece by piece in age-appropriate ways, your child will know when to call out for help and say, "This is wrong! Leave me alone!" One leader put it this way:

> Many "experts" today, in their rush to always make kids feel good about their sexuality and in their hesitancy to establish any moral norms whatsoever, recommend parental tolerance of even the most outrageous of childhood sexual experiences. This is unwise. Establishing clear norms for acceptable and unacceptable behavior for your children is part of protecting them. It's part of helping them enforce clear boundaries of protection for themselves. The best way to prevent abuse of your children is to build their character by giving them the beliefs, skills, and supportive environment that will best protect them.[11]

6

What Is Sex?

And this is my prayer: that your love may abound more and more
in knowledge and depth of insight, so that you may be able
to discern what is best and may be pure and blameless.

Philippians 1:9-10

The biggest oasis in the world is located in Saudi Arabia near the Persian Gulf. The al-Hasa oasis has been inhabited since ancient times and is the only water source in a vast arid region. It encompasses 30,000 acres and is surrounded by approximately three million date palms.

The oasis is a candidate for one of the seven natural wonders of Asia and is fed by more than 60 artesian wells. These wells nourish the economy through productive agricultural yields of date trees, rice, corn, and citrus fruits. In this lush setting you can also find herds of sheep, goats, cattle, camels, and even egg farms, making al-Hasa one of the major Saudi food producers. It is a life-sustaining oasis.

But by 1961 this lush oasis was in severe danger. Villagers sent an urgent appeal for help to the central government's Ministry of Agriculture—"The desert is upon us!" The wind was whipping across the vast desert, piling the sand upon the only sun-sheltered and safe place to inhabit for miles around—the oasis! At a rate of 30 feet each year, sand was ebbing away at the oasis and 14 villages were in immediate danger.

In the time span of a child growing up in the villages, the oasis could be destroyed by the power of the scorching hot carnage of desert sands.

In describing this desert, one authority says, "Wind, then, is the essential force in the creation and movement of dunes, and nowhere in the world does it have more freedom to mold and move mountains of sand than it does on the Arabian Peninsula. More than 1,000,000 square miles in area, the peninsula contains many great deserts, one of which, the Rub' al-Khali (The Empty Quarter), a basin some 400 by 700 miles in area, contains approximately 250,000 square miles of sand, the largest continuous body of sand in the world."[1] Without a plan to keep the sand out, the desert would overtake this life-giving oasis.

Many methods to contain the ever creeping desert were considered, but of all the technology available, the Supreme Planning Board of Saudi Arabia gave speedy approval for a plan to build a barrier, nine miles long, 150 feet wide, and studded with three million seedling trees. In addition, an ambitious irrigation system was laid in place to keep the trees watered, as well as provide canals, reservoirs, and above-ground viaducts to continue life uninterrupted in the oasis.

Trees planted along the water, in the desert, was the path to success. Sound familiar? It seems like we have heard this good wisdom before:

> Blessed is the one who does not walk in step with the wicked or stand in the way that sinners take or sit in the company of mockers, but whose delight is in the law of the LORD, and who meditates on his law day and night. That person is like a tree planted by streams of water, which yields its fruit in season and whose leaf does not wither— whatever they do prospers (Psalm 1:1-3).

Just as the oasis gives life to the desert, so providing an oasis to your child in the elementary years will give life to their future—if you can keep the desert of the evil one away from his or her life.

A Childhood Oasis

We call the time from ages six to eleven "the oasis" because it serves as a wide spot in the road, a calm place, a shade tree for replenishment and rest for your family. It is past the turbulent and often strenuous toddler and preschool years but before the hormones of teen life kick in. This makes it a relatively calm period in a child's life. It might be busy, but it can be an emotionally peaceful time. This is a wise time to do some teaching and preparation.

When I (Pam) was growing up on a farm, each summer it was my job to "roll bales." From as soon as I was able to push a hay bale over one quarter of a roll, I was recruited to walk the fields after the hay had been baled and push over the bales so no mold would gather and ruin the hay. I remember helping with this task as young as age seven or eight. It was a hot job in the scorching summer sun. But I loved it. I was a part of something important—helping my family produce some of the income we would live on during the cold winter months. This work also had a valuable upside as we spent precious family time together.

It was hot work, however, and halfway through the day we would have our own oasis of sorts. We'd all gather for an ample lunch of my grandmother's lip-smacking-good cooking. My favorite spot to enjoy the noon meal was under the big weeping willow on my grandparents' front lawn. It was a haven of peace and coolness. We all would linger long over good food and good conversation. Some of the best talks I ever had with the adults in my life—parents, grandparents, aunts, and uncles—came as we sat in the shade together. As I look back, so much wisdom passed from generation to generation as we reclined together in our own unique oasis.

Like the shade the weeping willow gave my family, you are the shade over your child's head as you train him for the path ahead. This vital season of life should be spent in preparation for the future. And just as the desert sands tried to steal the oasis of al-Hasa, the world and the ungodly forces of media, secular sex education, and dangerous predators will seek to encroach upon the safe shelter of the oasis time of your child's life.

We're going to look at five barriers that will keep the oasis of life in and the desert sands of Satan out! If you will nurture each area of your child's life, they will have all they need to handle the desert season of the teen years. During the teen years, kids wanting to make great choices often feel very alone, so to them it might feel like they are crossing a vast desert with no sight of the refreshing shores of adult-hood. The average boy spends thirteen years before puberty and then fourteen years after puberty before he marries, and the average young woman today spends twelve years before puberty and then thirteen more years as a sexually mature woman before she marries.[2] The oasis is short. Soon, hormones will begin to kick in and make your job as a parent a little harder. Protect and invest in the oasis years!

A Five-Sided Diamond

There are five sides to the barrier to protect your child, but it could also be said that there are five sides to a well-cut diamond. Your child's life will shine like a precious jewel as you nurture them in these five areas. Mark Laaser, author of *Talking to Your Kids About Sex*, describes healthy sexuality as having five dimensions.[3] We'll explore our view of these dimensions in detail as we continue. There is much to pass on to your children in these vital areas so we will take a few chapters to go over the important conversations, traditions, and plans to set in place during the oasis time. The areas we will look at are:

- Relational—understanding sexual intercourse
- Physical—understanding body changes
- Personal—understanding feelings
- Emotional—understanding body image
- Spiritual—understanding God's call of character

This means a smart parent will help a child get a strong foundation in each of these areas.

Puberty for the majority of girls hits between the ages of nine and eleven and for boys between ten and thirteen. This means you should plan the "big reveal" or "monumental moment" talk or talks with your daughter when she's eight and with your son when he's nine.

Relational—Understanding Sexual Intercourse

In this chapter we'll focus on the first facet of the diamond—teaching your child about the mechanics of sex. In the last chapter, you read about how to lay the first layer of sexual information into your child's life. Now it is time for the next "monumental moment." Before you feel the pressure and responsibility of "the big talk," just remember your kids have no idea how this talk is supposed to go or what a parent is expected to say, so you have a very easy-to-please audience. They want you to feel at ease in all your conversations with them, and this is no different. Take off the comparisons and expectations and park them in prayer with Jesus. After some solid preparation, pray something like, "Okay, God, we're ready. Help us to communicate the things You think are important in a way that helps our child feel close to You and close to us. Please allow us to communicate in a way that this will help them make wise choices for their future. We commit this time and our child to Your care and leading. Amen." Now exhale and relax!

The Timing

This is the time to give the "big reveal" talk so your son or daughter knows exactly what sex is and how the body mechanics fit together to create a baby. We decided to do the "big reveal" when we felt the need to explain menstruation to our sons (or for you, your daughters). We wanted our sons to be fully prepared to be gentlemen if their female classmates needed them to be. For example, if they saw feminine products in a girl's desk or her purse or if she said she couldn't swim or play some sport or game in PE, we wanted our guys to be prepared to handle the changes in their female friends. If we did our jobs as parents right, our son would *not* be the one to say, "What's this?" as he held up a feminine product. He would *not* be the one to say, "Why can't you swim? What's wrong with you?" He would *not* be the one to say to a girl, "There's something on your backside" or worse, "She has blood all over her seat!" Instead, we wanted our sons to be the ones who could say:

- "Leave her alone!" (if classmates were drawing negative attention to a girl)
- "Can I get the teacher for you?"
- "Can I get one of your friends for you?"
- "Can I get your purse?"
- "Want me to get you a snack while you sit here?"
- "Want to put your feet in the water? I will sit here with you for a while."
- "Here, take my jacket. You can wrap it around your waist."
- "Go out the door here; I will walk behind you so no one else sees the spot."
- "Want me to get the nurse for you?"
- "Can I go to the store for you?"

Acting on this preparation might start out as an awkward third grader who quietly walks up and whispers to his teacher, "I think Jenny might need your help. I saw blood on her chair and her shorts." But soon this same son will turn into the boy who wisely knows how to deflect attention so a girl can get to her purse or the bathroom and escape a crowd to care for an emergency. He'll become the date who plans a schedule in which trips to the bathroom are always convenient. Someday he'll be the husband who is brave and polite enough to buy feminine products with his favorite chips and dip at the grocery store.

In explaining menstruation even at this young age, you'll be able to tell your children about the fertilization of an egg, which then links to sexual intercourse and the godly timing of coitus to the marriage bed—and how to wait until then! Once the first domino it tapped, it is time to deal with the whole trail of dominos. Get ready to follow the rabbit trails as you communicate truth during the oasis. One topic leads to the next.

Linda and Richard Eyre, the authors of *How to Talk to Your Child About Sex*, suggest that the age of eight is a "window between the disinterest of very young childhood and the moodiness and unpredictability of pre-puberty." They go on:

> Most eight-year-olds are trusting, open, innocent, anxious to please, and fairly fascinated by the world around them. They simply haven't yet learned to be embarrassed, sarcastic or cynical...One of the greatest things about most seven- and eight-year-olds is their susceptibility to anticipation and excitement. Because of this it is possible to really pump them up, to build a positive and happy level of enthusiasm leading up to the "big talk." It is important to have your main discussion (and your pre- and follow-up discussions) early enough that they form your child's initial attitudes toward sex and serve as a deflector of all "silliness," "dirtiness" and nonsense children hear from friends, peers, and media. But having it too early raises issues that kids aren't ready for...
>
> ...Unless you have compelling reasons for starting earlier or unless your child is already older than eight, we suggest that you target and plan for the day or the week of the eighth birthday for "the big talk." Pegging it to a birthday can help build the desired kind of positive, excited anticipation. (It gives you a deadline so you won't put it off.) If your child is a little older than eight, pick or designate some other special day that is at least a few weeks in the future.[4]

It Takes a Team

Procreation takes both a man and a woman, but sometimes the truth of this in the first talk doesn't really click with a preschooler. This may be especially true if you paint the picture of conception with a broad brush, saying something like, "Mommy and Daddy loved each other in a special way, like God created married couples to do." Even if you are a little more specific, you likely cared more about the precise words and details than your preschooler did. To him or her it might have seemed like a sweet day, a wonderful picture book, but probably not as mammoth in his or her mind and memory as it was yours! Be flexible and allow the conversation to flow. The conversation should be like a tennis match, batting the ball back and forth over the net as you share and ask questions.

With this talk, containing all the details of just how the plumbing fits together and why, the pieces of the puzzle often fall together for a child. The "aha!" moment often hits and the lightbulb of understanding goes on. Here's how one of Linda and Richard Eyres' daughters describes the experience of this big talk and her realization of the father's importance in the process:

> When I was seven years old, I began to wonder why fathers seemed to be an integral part of so many families. I had several younger brothers and sisters, so I'd seen my mother's protruding belly with each new child and I had felt the unborn baby kick around in there when I placed my hand on my mother's tummy. I had a basic understanding of the fact that babies come out of their mothers. But I didn't get how fathers fit into the picture. I loved my dad—he was a whole lot of fun, but was he necessary? What made me distinctly his daughter rather than someone else's daughter? How was I really connected to him?…My eighth birthday finally rolled around…They not only told me about the basic "plumbing" of sex, they told me that it was a wonderful, special thing that two people who loved each other could share. I don't remember the exact words they used, but I remember the basic feeling of the message, and it was good and warm.[5]

Once she heard the details of the "oasis" time at age eight, Dad's role suddenly became vital, so Dad himself became more important in her eyes. These are the kind of fundamental elements you are seeking to sow in your child's heart at this early stage. Those seeds will reap positive dividends later on in his or her life. Making time for these talks will be worth it later on, Mom and Dad.

What to Say

If age eight is the next platform stop on the subway train toward healthy sexuality, what are some suggested conversations and topics to go over at this oasis station? Often parents stress about saying either too little or too much too early. Mark Laaser puts those worries to rest:

> The question of how old is old enough to hear about the biology of genital sexuality is a highly controversial subject, particularly in the Christian community. Many parents are afraid if they tell their children about sex, they will become sexual. On the contrary, every piece of research I have seen suggests that the less kids know about sex, the more likely they are to experiment with it.[6]

Many parents begin with picture books to introduce very young children to the concept of sex. We recommend being very picky about what picture book you use to make sure it matches your value system. Some are very permissive and encourage children to be secretive. Other books endorse every form of sexual expression without any guidelines reflecting faith, God, or moral restraint. A trip to a local bookstore where you can scan through scores of books might be helpful, or use an online bookstore that has plenty of sample pages you can read before you order. The best option is to find a ministry or leader you trust and see what he or she has available on the topic. Be sure to pre-read and pre-watch any books or videos before you use them with your child.

It was important to us that sex was framed as appropriate in a committed, loving marriage. We were always sure to use the term "making love" *only* in the context of marriage. (All other sex is "making lust.") There are many books and videos to choose from. We encourage you to buy several and then piece together a plan to explain sex the way you are most comfortable and the way you want your child to learn about it.

Getting Started

We also try to ease into the discussion of sexual mechanics with a warm-up, say, a dinner out, a fun activity, or even just an ice cream cone. We tended to make these "talks" along life's trail special moments.

If the child is alone with his or her parents, away from siblings, that alone might make the date special! We liked to set a comfortable mood by enjoying a desired activity or sharing a meal of the child's favorite food. Then we would look for a private place to talk. Some restaurants are conducive, and other times we went to the park or even back home (with siblings elsewhere) before we would initiate the conversation. Give plenty of time for this talk and interaction. There is much to discuss and much for the child to digest! We suggest a four- to six-hour time frame so you can relax and enjoy the time and not feel rushed. After some fun, you can begin the conversation with something like:

"Remember this book?" Pull out the picture book that had first introduced them to the idea of sex. "Well, there is another book in this series that explains more about the special hug that moms and dads do when they are married. Let's read it together."

After the child has taken time to read the book and you've discussed the material together, wrap up with something like:

"Sex is a beautiful special hug because it is how God creates a new life—a new baby. And new babies are a gift from God. Sex is a special gift from God. It feels very good to be loved this way so God saved it for the most special of all relationships—marriage. God planned sex to bring people very, very close and help them feel they are one. God said this kind of love shows the world God's love because it is based on a lifelong commitment. A commitment is a promise that is always kept and never broken. That is how God loves us: He always keeps His promises. He wants us to not make promises we cannot keep, and that is why sex is supposed to be given when you love someone so much you marry them. Then the gift you give each other as a wedding present is sex. When people love each other God's way, they feel cherished and protected. They create a new family that is strong and stable. So do you think God sees sex as very, very special? If God thinks sex is very special, do you think He wants us to feel it is very, very special too?" Wait for their answer.

"Yes, He does. And that's why God wants us to protect sex with marriage. God wants us to keep our promise and save sex for marriage. That is why some people call sex "making love" because when you love someone so much you want to marry them, you can unwrap the gift of sex.

"So let's see if you understand what sex is. We'll ask you some questions and then you can ask us anything you're wondering about, okay?

"Can you explain sex to us in your own words?" Wait for an answer. You might need to help him or her out to summarize all they have taken in.

"Why is sex a special gift?

"Who are the only people that God says should enjoy this special gift of sex?

"Will you show your love for God and wait until marriage to give this special gift of sex?

"Do you have any questions about what sex is?" (Wait to see if your child can think of any questions.)

The last part of the conversation might sound like:

"Do you think all people keep their promise to save sex just for the person they marry?" Wait for an answer.

"That's right—sometimes people do not keep their promise of love. Some people do not cherish sex as God's very special gift so they have sex with many people. Because this is not God's perfect plan for the special gift of sex, many sad things can happen. If you have sex before you are married, you can get diseases, and some of those diseases can make it so you cannot ever have a baby or some can even make you die. Or sometimes if someone has sex with you but they don't marry you, your heart is broken and you can get very, very sad. Sometimes having sex before you get married means a baby comes and that baby doesn't have both a mommy and a daddy living in the same house. That's hard on a baby. Sometimes a daddy will just leave a mommy and then the mommy and the baby can become poor and not have enough money to live on. Some men sometimes don't value a woman and they push themselves on her when she doesn't want to have sex. This is called rape and it is breaking the law and you can go to jail for it. So many sad things happen when people do not treat sex like God's special gift. We will talk about many of these things another time, little by little, but tonight, Mom and Dad just want you to know how very special sex is, and that it is the most special, cherished, amazing gift you will ever give and ever receive from the person you will marry someday.

"Do you have any questions?" Wait for an answer, and give honest responses to anything your child asks.

"Can you remember any of the sad things that can happen if people don't listen to God and use sex for their own selfish reasons instead of as a special gift they should only give their husband or wife?" Wait for an answer.

"We believe you are smart enough, courageous enough, and love God and yourself enough to wait to unwrap the gift of sex on your wedding night. Do you think you are that wise, smart, and brave?" Wait for an answer. "Do you think you love us, God, and yourself enough to follow God's plan for sex and wait until you are married like God has planned so He can bless you and your marriage like this?" Wait for an answer.

"We agree—and we are so proud of you because you want to love and obey God. God is proud of you too, and He will bless you for this wise choice. If you keep choosing God's plan you will see just how wonderful and amazing this gift of sex is."

If appropriate, this is where you can add your endorsement, like, "Mom and Dad have been married for ___ years and we still think sex is God's special amazing gift. Grandma and Grandpa have been married for ___ years and they think God had a good idea when He came up with the gift of sex. When you get married, we think you will agree that God did a good thing when He invented sex. It is worth the wait."

Then we shift gears from the gift of sex to the changes that are ahead for them. We'll share more about puberty in the next chapter.

Handling Their Pushback

If a child expresses any negative feedback (and it is natural to do so), Stan and Brenna Jones suggest this kind of conversation. Take note of the word picture toward the end of the talk:

> *Child:* So that's sex? When people talk about having sex, they mean a man's penis being in a woman's vagina? That's so gross!

Parent: I know, I felt the same way you do when I first heard about sex. I think maybe God makes us in such a way that when we're too young to have sex, it just sounds gross to us. But it really isn't gross. Someday, when you really love someone and are physically ready to have sex, it won't sound gross anymore. Instead it will sound wonderful. I remember when your mom and I were dating, I wanted to have sex with her. But even when it sounds lovely, it isn't the right thing to do until you are married. God wants you to have sex only with your husband [or wife]. Since your mom and I weren't married, we didn't.

Child: Why does God have that rule?

Parent: Well, like we read in this book, God made sex as a special gift for husbands and wives to share only with each other. You know how you feel about your most special toys—you really don't like to share them? Well, sex is a little like that. It isn't meant to be shared with anyone but your husband (or wife). To share it with other people would ruin it. It is like two radios that two people can use to talk just to each other. If you break the radios into more pieces so that three or six people can share all the pieces, the radios are broken and don't work. They were not meant to be shared like that.

Child: Oh.

Parent: You know what? I like talking with you about this and I am glad that you want to know. Would you please tell me when you have more questions so that I can talk more with you about this? Sex is very beautiful, but a lot of people believe wrong things about it, so you will hear other kids telling you really dumb and wrong stuff. And television will show you many people who have wrong ideas about sex. So I want to talk with you about it so that you will know God's truth about sex.[7]

The above conversation uses several great teaching techniques:

- Affirm that their feelings are normal

- Stay calm yourself
- Link the subject to a time in your own life
- Link it to a word picture that is at their developmental level
- Offer to answer any future questions
- Reaffirm that God's plan is positive, beautiful, and intended to have their best interest at heart

Explain a Lot…But Not Everything

For this special night, try to keep the main thing the main thing: *God made sex and sex is good when used as God intended.* We waited until the next "monumental moment" just before junior high to explain things like homosexuality, cross-dressing, and other perversions and fetishes—and even then we tried to keep the conversation G-rated to spare them from any trauma or negative images being seared into their minds. If topics presented themselves, we would address them as they came up.

In the next chapters, we will explain some of the vital topics you will need to discuss in today's sex-saturated world and how a child should best handle things like feelings toward the same sex, people who identify themselves as homosexual, how to handle pornography if he comes across it, the truth about abortion, and how to protect themselves against sexual predators. On the "big reveal" night, we tried, for the most part, to keep this monumental moment positive, focused on the "rightness" of how God created sex and what He intended for sex. We dealt with most of the negatives a little later in this stage (as we saw things on TV, heard news reports, or had people in our world who were dealing with some of the unintended consequences of using sex outside of God's plan). For tonight, for this one brief, special moment, we wanted the splendor and wonder of sex as God intended to play center-stage in our child's heart and mind.

Answers to Have Ready

Selecting the book or video to relay God's most "special gift" is one of the most important decisions you will make as a parent. In addition to the guidelines suggested in this chapter so far, when we were looking for book and videos, we wanted to make sure the most important topics were covered. Here is the list of items we wanted any book or video to include for this "big reveal" moment. Feel free to use or adapt this list as you go shopping for the best resource for your child's oasis talk. We wanted the book or video to include tactful drawings explaining body parts of both genders and we wanted an easy-to-understand explanation of sexual interaction that would include specifics like:

- The act of intercourse explained specifically but tactfully (a father placing his penis inside the mother's vagina).

- The sperm from the father swimming up the vagina, uterus, and Fallopian tubes to find the egg in a woman's womb.

- The sperm connecting with the egg of a mother to create a baby (called an embryo).

- That a baby is not made every time a man and a woman make love, but it is possible anytime they make love. Only God knows which times the egg and the sperm will match and connect perfectly to create a baby.

- That the embryo is a baby from the moment of conception and it just needs time and care to grow to look like what we think of as a baby.

- The baby is attached to the mother through the umbilical cord. That is how a baby gets the nutrients to grow.

- Photos or drawings of a real baby in the womb at various sizes through his or her growth.

- After nine months that baby would be ready to be born.

- When it is time to be born, God makes a woman's body feel contractions that squeeze on the womb to help the baby move down the birth canal.

- The baby exits the womb through the cervix, a special opening between the mother's legs.

- The baby is welcomed into a loving family.

- What happens when the egg is not fertilized by the father's sperm (the menstrual cycle).
- The changes that happen in a boy and a girl during puberty.
- When to expect puberty.
- What sexual feelings to expect.
- That sex is meant for marriage.

And we wanted any pictures or photos to show people happy about God's amazing gift of sex and procreation. We sought out resources that were very pro-life, pro-marriage, pro-family responsibility, and pro-God. Biblical references or verses were an additional plus that we looked for as well.

Parent to Parent

You will likely get into discussions with other parents over the right time for the "big reveal" talk. Here are some of the reasons why we think age eight is a good time:

Eight is good timing for the big talk because it lands *before* so many vital markers: before puberty begins, hopefully before they hear about sex from others at school, before they experiment or get sexual feelings pressuring them internally, before your daughter menstruates, before your son has a wet dream. Eight is likely also before any detailed sex education is given in your school system.

Eight is also a good time because it is *after* your child has learned some basic anatomy from you and at school. It is after he or she learns to read so they can read along with you any resource you select or they can continue to read on their own any resources you might give to him or her. Eight is also after the cognitive change in learning where more abstract thinking kicks in (so they can picture in their mind what you are describing, even with few pictures or none at all as they engage their imagination).

Eight is also after many religions mark early faith decisions and give more responsibilities to a child in their own spiritual journey. (For example: The Catholic Church celebrates a child's first communion at age seven or eight. In smaller evangelical congregations, the children's ministry often ends at second or third grade and children aged eight or nine are invited into the adult worship service.) Many parents, philosophers, and theologians believe it is sometime in middle elementary years that a child can comprehend the gospel and explain it in their own words. This is the time in childhood when the Christmas story moves to center around the manger and not Santa and presents and Easter is more about the cross than the Easter bunny. The child's conscience and inner moral compass is engaged, so moral lessons and not just biology can be integrated into the big talk.

Answers for Your Heart

It is vital that you as a parent pray through your own childhood experiences when it comes to the topic of sex. You will want to keep the thoughts and actions that were healthy and replace those that were unhealthy in the way you were educated (or not) about sex. Stan and Brenna Jones encourage parents to confront their child's sexuality—and their own:

> Parents can't do anything to stop their children from being sexual. If…[Mom] were to respond negatively to her child for being sexual (spanking him, rejecting him by withholding attention, or some other form of punishment), the trauma to her child would be significant. She would be punishing him for being how God made him—a sexual child. She would be teaching him to repress or reject an aspect of himself that God gave him as a gift. At these earliest ages, the child needs no verbal comment or particular response from the parent. [The child] doesn't even know he has a penis! But he can sense whether [Mom] loves him or if she is hesitant, withdrawn or rejecting. Early on is the time for you to work on your own responses to the child's sexuality. When you are changing diapers, look at your child's genitals and say a prayer of thanksgiving that God made that child sexual. Be honest with yourself and God about any ambivalent feelings you have. Resolve to

do something about those feelings by reading, praying or talking to someone who can help.[8]

Take time to do an inventory of your own childhood and when sexuality was awakened in you. Pull out your journal and answer these few questions by completing the writing prompts:

- Dear God, when I first heard about sex I felt…
- I believe that was (too early, too late, at just the right time)…
- God, I remember my first sexual feelings were…
- I believe they were (accurate, unhealthy, confusing, other)…
- I believe my parents' attitude toward sex in general and in their own marriage was (healthy, neutral, unhealthy)…
- The comfort level of my parents talking to me about sex was (healthy and happy, unhealthy, shaded by their own pain, nonexistent, a little awkward)…
- Some things I think my parents did right to help me make good choices about morality and sexuality:
- Some things my parents should have done differently that might have saved me from hurt, harm, confusion, or making poor choices later in life:
- When I talk to my kids I want to remember to…

7

What's Happening to My Body?

Your eyes saw my unformed body; all the days ordained for me
were written in your book before one of them came to be.

Psalm 139:16

Love Being a Girl! was a rite of passage for all the fourth graders in my public school. The youngsters, all dressed in their prettiest feminine dresses and shiny leather shoes, excitedly joined the fifth- and sixth-grade girls for this "Girl's Day." The faculty smiled as they welcomed us and then showed a film on menstruation that made many of us grab our tummies in disbelief and fear. The adults tried to take the edge off by giving all the girls some free sanitary pads and cookies. The older girls took the cookies; the younger girls ran for their mothers. The assembly was at the end of the school day so the freaked-out girls could at least travel home with their moms and debrief. (We are glad some kind of education is offered, but it is so much better for parents to be the first educator and then use any educational programs to back up what you have already shared. It is emotionally hard to be surprised by the explanation as you face all the facts and all your peers at once.)

I couldn't help but be anxious the first time I saw the film. There was blood involved! But I was also relieved and comforted to learn that tampons would allow me to keep swimming, dancing, and doing gymnastics even when I was on my period. I remember feeling grateful for scientists, who, I was sure, had to be very smart women.

When I was in sixth grade and my little sister in fourth, her response was very different. After the movie, she skipped past the cookies and ran to the car. I ran after her because she was so pale I feared she might pass out on the way. When Mom got in the car, my sister shouted, "I hate being a girl! It's not fair! I will *not* do that! I will not bleed and I will never get married and I will never have a baby—I refuse! I want to be a boy! This girl thing is too hard!"

My mother tried to calm my sister. "But sweetie, you love babies. You are a wonderful babysitter. Someday you will want children of your own to love."

With arms crossed over her chest as if to keep breasts from developing, my sister huffed out, "Then I will adopt!"

"That's definitely an option. But let's just give it some time. You might change your mind. Once you fall in love, love kind of changes everything."

My sister retorted, "If I have to have sex I will never *ever* fall in love!" At this point my mother and I were both holding back the giggles… but then my sister burst into tears and uncontrollable sobs. I patted her back and gave her a big "it will be all right" hug.

Mom also tried to comfort my sister as she drove. "Once you are married, you might change your mind. But you have a long time until then, so let's just help you get through your first menstrual period."

"Can I go to the doctor and put that off—like 'til I'm a hundred?"

"No, honey, you can't put it off, and not for that long, but it will be a few more years before you start—probably. Now, shall we go for ice cream?"

"Okay." The ice cream did calm her—or at least distract her. She had three years from that dreadful day to get used to the idea of menstruation before she actually had to deal with it. When she started getting curvy and all the boys in her class were falling all over themselves to give her attention, having a period suddenly became a small price to pay. And she did eventually fall in love, marry, and have children—and she was much younger than 100 when it happened!

Yes, body changes can feel traumatic! But they can also feel great!

Our middle son, Zach, went through an awkward, pudgy stage from about ages 10 to 13. Peers are merciless at this stage so we worked hard to bolster Zach's self-image. I knew from experience that puberty can eventually transform a person struggling with "baby fat." My own brother went from roly-poly doughboy to growing 12 inches in less than a year! We just had to wait for testosterone to kick in. We looked for a place where Zach could excel and we found a haven for him in extreme sports. The boy was fearless on a skateboard or a bike. We kept him active and begged God to send the magical mighty testosterone quickly! Finally, in Zach's freshman year of high school he went from fifth string on a football team to starting Varsity in one season! He went from awkward to an adult. Yes, puberty can be a cruel master or a beloved friend!

If you carefully prepare your child, puberty is a little easier to process. There will still be a lot of emotion along with it, but a good plan can help your son or daughter survive the roller coaster ride of body changes. Let's look at the remaining areas of change to prepare for.

Physical: Understanding Body Changes

There are two choices in the "big reveal talk." After explaining clearly what sex is, you can continue to explain body changes (you are on a roll, so just keep surfing the wave) or you can set another time later in the year to plan a fun activity and teach your children about the rest of the equation: body changes.

You might wonder, *Why talk about body changes at the same time as the big reveal of what sex is? Won't our son or daughter have a dazed look or intake overload?* Perhaps. But we have seen that usually one topic leads to the other and the questions are naturally right on the surface, so you can begin dealing with them at the same time.

You might transition the conversation from "What is sex?" to changes in an adult's body with something like:

"Because sex is worth the wait, God takes His time preparing your body. Your body is made by God to get ready for marriage. As you get older there will be some changes in your body. Mom doesn't look like the girls in your class, does she? And Dad doesn't look like the boys in your class, does he? That is because everyone goes through a special change that God also created. It's called *puberty*. Let's go over those changes one by one then you can ask us any questions you have about the ways your body is changing." Then go over all the changes of puberty first in your child's gender, then in the opposite gender. We took a little bit of a "divide and conquer" approach. After we did the big reveal, we let that information sit as we planned the next layer of puberty teaching. This time we each took a piece. Bill planned a time away (typically on his yearly father-son trip), and I planned a "date with mom." Bill would explain all the changes our son would have happen in his body in puberty. I explained all the changes that happen in a girl's life and prepared them to be gentlemen, handling well this "insider information" he now owned.

Change Is Good

Let's go over the physical changes you will want to enlighten your child about.

Your Son

When our sons were about ten or eleven, we would give them either for a birthday or Christmas, a shaving kit. Now we knew they would not shave for a few years. However, we gave the personal toiletry kit to signal to our sons that they were moving from little boy status to manhood. They definitely needed the toiletry kit, and as a parent you will know when to give it! Sometime between eight and ten boys really start to stink up the place! Whew! The body odors can get downright rank. In the toiletry bag we included items like deodorant, foot spray, body soap, and men's cologne or body spray. We also added in a manicure set, pumice stone, callous file, and nose hair clippers. We placed it all in a very cool bag with an invitation to use this overnight kit on an adventure with Dad.

While they may or may not be excited about the kit, they will be thrilled with the time planned around something they love to do! But they do need the kit! Boys at this age really try to avoid personal care.

Heaven to them is a place with no showers and plenty of dirt, some frogs, snakes, hammers, nails, any kind of a ball, maybe some video games, trading cards, and anything with wheels that can go *fast!* And boys have one deep love—food! Girls, for the most part, are not their top priority.

Early in the oasis time, girls are "the enemy" and boys seek to win any competition with them at all costs. But there comes a day when all this changes, and it seems to sneak up on you as a parent overnight! For example, one year when our son Caleb was going into sixth grade, we were speaking at Cannon Beach Christian Conference Center. We began the week with a son who thought it was a waste of time to take a shower because, after all, "I go in the ocean every day." Then we started hearing about his pal, Sam, who he had met in the children's program. Seems Sam was great at basketball, pretty talented at throwing a football, and winning footraces and game time competitions. One day Caleb said, "Hey, can we go to the bonfire tonight and make s'mores? Sam's family is going."

We should have been clued in because Caleb took a shower, did his hair—with gel—and wore his clean gym shorts and clean sweatshirt. You guessed it. We showed up and met *Samantha* and her family! (Sam was beautiful, godly, and, yes, very athletic, but we could tell Caleb's admiration for her was for things other than her ability to throw a spiral!) Caleb had been preening like a peacock in front of every mirror in our room. We had both noticed that Caleb had been looking at his reflection more often as we passed by plate glass windows and checking the size of his biceps—a sure sign that a boy on the brink of manhood has discovered the appeal of the opposite gender!

The Changing Landscape of Manhood

There are many changes coming for your son as puberty hits, and it's best to make him aware of them early on:

- Get taller
- Shoulders broaden
- Muscles enlarge and strengthen

- Perspiration increases in amount and odor
- Skin and hair get oilier
- Arms and legs get hairier
- Hair grows in pubic area and under arms
- Pimples or acne can appear
- Voice begins to change; it may "crack" as it lowers
- Penis and scrotum grow larger
- More spontaneous erections occur
- Wet dreams or nocturnal emissions can occur
- Sexual feelings begin
- May experiment with masturbation

I (Pam) remember looking down at each son's legs and feet and thinking—*he's a man!* Gone are the pudgy toes and smooth legs and in their place are man feet and hairy legs! At this same time pubic hair grows in and there will be hair appearing on his upper lip, chin, and maybe some initial sideburns as well as hair under his armpits. While their body is changing, their view of themselves as an adult is latent, yet to be developed or embraced. It is wise for a father or the men in your son's world to talk to him and treat him as a young man.

An honest conversation needs to happen man-to-man about wet dreams being normal and how to handle the spontaneous erection that might occur when thoughts drift to something sexual. (We will deal with pornography and masturbation in another chapter, and this might be a good time to talk over the important mind-body connection and how a son can guard his heart and mind, thus guarding his own sexual future.)

Your Daughter

I (Pam) thought it was a humorous day but neither my neighbor, who was my age, or her ten-year-old daughter were laughing. Kristie, the daughter, was often at my home because I had a new baby who she loved to play with. She was a terrific mother's helper. However, this day all she seemed to do was complain about her mom. "She's so grumpy! She's so bossy! I can never please her! She's always picking on me!" I spent the morning encouraging Kristie to give her mom the benefit of the doubt and a liberal helping of love and grace. When I got my baby down for a nap, Kristie said she needed to go home because her "witch of a mom" (her words) left the dishes for her to do. "I'm just like Cinderella—but without the ball gown!" She dragged herself across the street and I went to my computer to write.

I had barely written a paragraph when her mom, Karen, opened my front door. "Yoohoo, friend! Are you home? I brought mocha!"

I gave her a hug and before I could sit down with the mug, Karen let loose. "I just don't know what's up with Kristie. She used to be such a nice daughter! I don't even know her! She is moody, whines all the time, is talking back, and is so lethargic. She used to be such a help around the house but just now she said I was treating her like a Cinderella slave! It's like I have a teenager in the house...but she's just ten!"

I smiled and gave Karen a sympathetic hug.

"She's ten," I acknowledged. "Seems like her figure has been changing. Has she started her period?"

Karen let out a long sigh. "No, not yet. But that gives me hope!"

"Hope? Menstruation is hope?" I said, puzzled.

"Yeah. When her period starts at least I can track the moodiness and it will just be once a month, not every day! Wow, I am glad I came over—I bet all this drama is just the buildup before the menstruation flood."

"I think you might be tracking on this," I concurred.

"I can't even be angry with her bad behavior because I recognize myself in some of it. The PMS flu is what I like to call it."

"Yeah, it does take a while to learn how to control our emotions during PMS," I added.

"Control them! No, I indulge them. Isn't that why God created bubble baths, dark chocolate, and spas?"

We both laughed and then prayed for Kristie, and we continued to chat about creative ways to welcome her into the wonderful world of womanhood.

The Changing Landscape of Womanhood

In puberty a girl:

- Begins to gain curves
- Might also gain some weight
- Sees her breasts grow and they might become tender
- Observes hair growing in pubic region and under her armpits
- Grows hair on legs or a slight fuzz on her upper lip
- Could develop acne or pimples
- Has growth of her labia and it gets redder in color
- May sense spontaneous lubrication in her vagina
- Experiences the beginning of menstruation (typically about a year after her breasts begin to grow)
- Also experiences cramps, moodiness, headaches, fatigue, and other PMS-type symptoms
- May experiment with masturbation
- Begins having sexual feelings

Personal: Understanding Feelings

While the oasis is a calm time for the emotions, it is a little like sailing on a lake. At any moment the wind can whip up and everything changes! Hormones can rage and tweens hitting puberty become unrecognizable! In *Got Teens?* co-author Jill Savage and I (Pam) describe these changes:

> Dr. Jay Giedd of the National Institute of Health has been conducting a 13-year study into the mind of teens...[and has] discovered some interesting insights. Researchers once believed that a child's brain was nearly complete by age 12, but Dr. Giedd has discovered what all of us [parents] of teens have known all along—they aren't all grown-up yet!

(He might have also experienced this at home—he has four teens too!) The good doctor found that the brain undergoes dramatic changes well past puberty. The medical community is looking at how brain development might impact those traits we as [parents] are so aware of: emotional outbursts, reckless risk taking, rule breaking, and toying with things like sex, drugs, and alcohol.

...The brain seems to develop from back to front... "The very last part of the brain to be pruned and shaped to its adult dimensions is the prefrontal cortex, home of the so-called executive functions—planning, setting priorities, organizing thoughts, suppressing impulses, weighing the consequences of one's actions. In other words, the final part of the brain to grow up is the part capable of deciding, I'll finish my homework and take out the garbage, and *then* I'll IM my friends about seeing a movie."

According to UCLA neuroscientist Elizabeth Sowell, "Scientists and the general public had attributed the bad decisions teens make to hormonal changes, but once we started mapping where and when the brain changes were happening, we could say, Aha, the part of the brain that makes a teenager more responsible is not finished maturing yet."

The brain matures on a schedule, even with the onset of early or late hormonal puberty. Dr. Ronald Dahl, a psychiatrist at the University of Pittsburgh calls this the "tinderbox of emotions" because feelings hit a flashpoint more easily, but teens also tend to seek out situations where they can allow their emotions and passions to run wild. "Adolescents are actively looking for experiences to create intense feelings. It's a very important hint that there is some particular hormone-brain relationship contributing to the appetite for thrills, strong sensations and excitement."

"The parts of the brain responsible for things like sensation-seeking are getting turned on in big ways around the time of puberty," says Temple University psychologist Laurence Steinberg, "but the parts for exercising judgment are still maturing throughout adolescence. So you've got this time gap between when things impel kids toward taking risks early in adolescence, and when things allow people to think before they act come online. It's like turning on the engine of a car without a skilled driver at the wheel."

And do you ever wonder why teens misread your emotions and say, "Don't yell at me!" or "Why are you always mad at me?" There is a reason for that too. In a series of tests by Harvard, kids and adults were both asked to identify emotions displayed in a set of photographs. "In doing these tasks, kids and young adolescents rely heavily on the amygdala, a structure in the temporal lobes associated with emotional and gut reactions. Adults, rely...more on the frontal lobe, a region associated with planning and judgment." Adults made few errors assessing the pictures, but kids under 14 tended to make more mistakes. Young teens frequently misread emotions and place anger and hostility where none exists.

And why do teens do more stupid things when with friends than when they're alone? Yep, science has an explanation for that too! In a driving simulator, when teens and adults were asked to make a decision to run a yellow light or not, both made wise choices when playing the game alone. Teenagers, however, took more risks when playing the game with a group of friends. Statistics show that most teen crimes occur when kids are in a gang or with friends. And it isn't just peer pressure that makes a teen vulnerable to sex, drugs, and alcohol experimentation. Rapid changes in the dopamine-rich areas of the brain make them more at risk to the addictive effects of these factors.

Why is it so hard to get your teens off the sofa to take out the trash? Their nucleus accumbens, a region in the frontal cortex that directs motivation and reward seeking—you got it—is still under development! James Bork at the National Institute on Alcoholism explains, "If adolescents have a motivational deficit, it may mean that they are prone to engaging in behaviors that have either a really high excitement factor, or a really low effort factor, or a combination of both." His suggestion to us…is this: "When presenting suggestions, anything that parents can do to emphasize more immediate payoffs will be more effective." For example, telling your teen son that if he drinks he will be kicked off the football team is more impacting than telling him he may end up on skid row.

And there is a reason you find yourself waiting up for your teen. Their melatonin levels rise slower, so their "nighttime" comes later. For years, studies have…shown that teens learn better later in the day. And they really do need more sleep as their body is changing drastically, so letting them sleep in on occasion on the weekend might make you all happier![1]

And their sexual feelings are also awakened with a flip of the built-in hormonal switch. Mark Laaser explains it this way:

The physical dimension of healthy sexuality assumes that sexual desire is a God-given part of our biology, that there is a natural biological basis to our sexual feelings…Physical desire is built into the chemistry of our brains. We need to have it because it is the life force that drives us to reproduce and keep humankind from extinction…sexual desire and sexual response are intended by God, in the context of a loving marriage, for procreation and pleasure. We should never be afraid or ashamed of natural attraction or desire… at the same time, we must explain [to our children] that our natural brain chemistry is not intended to drive us like mere animals. Biblically, going back to the Garden of Eden, it is the work of the devil that takes human desire and turns it into selfish demand for immediate gratification. God, also, therefore, has created us with a spirit and has given us a set of instructions that can help us override our biological chemistry, a matter that requires discipline and practice. We need to teach our children that while it is normal to have sexual desire, people must learn to focus their desire on one person.[2]

Emotional: Understanding Body Image

Both boys and girls will be uncomfortable initially with all the morphing their body will be going through. Your daughter will be struggling to adjust to menstrual cramps, headaches, and feeling like she has the flu every 28 days. She may also feel self-conscious and have anxiety during her period, wondering if her "secret" will be exposed in an embarrassing way if a leak should occur. She will need to handle feeling more mature as she grows breasts or deal with feelings of inferiority if she is a late bloomer or if nature doesn't endow her with the same sized bosoms as her friends. She may gain weight and feel fat and unattractive. This can lead to anorexia or bulimia. In addition, her skin may be blotching up with acne. Life might appear unfair if she feels like an ugly duckling at the same time as she is beginning to be interested in boys.

If she is an early bloomer, she might be getting unwanted relationship attention. The expectation peers and others have on her might be beyond her inner maturity, even though her body says otherwise. Girls who mature early often get attention from older boys and feel ill-prepared for their advances. A wise parent will be close at hand to reassure her and equip her in the constantly shifting social changes that accompany her body changes. Teach your daughter to value modesty and dress to cover the 3 Bs: breasts, bottom, and belly. There are even fashion ministries that show "modest is hottest!"

The Guys Have Feelings Too

Boys, because they tend to mature later, may begin to feel inferior as girls start to pass them in height, the ability to communicate, or their ability to navigate the social circles. If your son is a late bloomer physically, just seeing (let alone showering after PE with) other boys and their bulging muscles will be a blow to his fragile ego. On the other hand, if he is an early bloomer, the days of enjoying the activities or expectations of a little boy are long gone. People will expect him to act like a man if he looks like one. Young men who mature early may experience a bravado and confidence that can turn a sweet boy into a bossy jerk. A boy can grow to enjoy the power nature has handed to him, and he will need to be instructed on how to best use his physical benefits in a God-honoring way.

Celebrate!

To help young men and women navigate puberty, we suggest looking for ways to equip and celebrate them as they face the changes that are coming their way. By weaving fun and new experiences together with your advice and life lessons, you can expand a child's and a teen's ability to receive your wisdom and the advice of mentors you might also want to invite into your son or daughter's life. By being proactive and planning a few key memory-making activities, you gain a window to speak truth into his or her life. You also give the message that you care, are clued in, and are the best person for them to talk with if any questions or issues arise.

We encourage you to leave your trademark (TM) on your child's heart with *traditions* and *memories*. Traditions are things that happen year after year to reinforce core principles. Memories are those once-in-a-lifetime events that mark a moment or drive a point home.

Rites of Passage

We believe it's important to celebrate the milestones in your child's life. Here are some rite of passage ideas you can use in the pre-puberty years up through young adulthood.

Marking Manhood

Man of Honor: Give your son two gifts: a sword to hang on the wall and a new Bible to remind your young man to turn to the sword of the Spirit, the Bible, for strength as he serves the King of kings. You might even include a "knighting" ceremony! This can be done at any age—from 12 up through 21. You choose the moment of manhood you want to mark. Inviting important men to participate extends your message into your young man's life through voices that echo your values.

Draft Card Dinner: Use registering for the draft as a way to mark manhood. If he is old enough to die for his country, he is definitely a man. Celebrate him and give gifts to help him be even more responsible: a briefcase, a business card holder, his own checking account, etc.

Walk into Manhood: Counselor Earl Henslin shared a tradition with us that we have incorporated in each of our son's lives as they headed off to college. (It also can be done for eighteenth birthdays or graduation.) Mentors, family members like grandparents and uncles, and older male friends and role models (coaches, schoolteachers, youth group leaders) are invited to a special celebration in honor of the eighteen-year-old. Before the event, the honoree is taken to a designated spot. It can be a forest trail, a lakeside, a beach, or even a track. The male members of the family have been given designated spots to stand along the trail. The father and son walk the first mile (or less) together and Dad imparts any last words of advice. He shares what he believes is the meaning of manhood with his son. Each man, in turn, walks and talks, imparting words of wisdom, affirmation, and a gift needed in adult life. At the trail end, all the men gather and pray over this young man as he enters adulthood.

For our oldest, a quarterback, we used a football field as he was going off to college to play football. For our middle son, it was a drive into manhood at a racecar track. Our youngest son is now planning his. As he is an outdoorsman and an athlete, it might be a kayak ride into manhood or a mountain climb into manhood. Each mentor brings a quote or a Bible verse to go in a scrapbook. We take a picture with each mentor and add in their addresses and phone numbers, ensuring that our sons will have plenty of wise mentors to call on if they need some guidance or advice in the journey ahead.

Shaving Rituals: Giving a tween or early teen all the goods for shaving when his voice begins to crack is a nice touch (as we have already mentioned). But a nice addition to the gift would be to accompany the present with a meal out with "the men" of the family: older brothers, dad, uncles, grandpa, etc. Each person can share a story starting, "I knew I was a man when…"

Welcoming Womanhood

Here are a few ways to celebrate your daughter and her step across some of the thresholds into womanhood:

Modern-Day Princess: In this rite of passage, a mom or a mentor walks a tween or teen girl through seven weeks of preparation in areas such as friendships, relationships with parents and mentors, makeup and manners, what God says about boys and men, how to grow with God, how to serve others, and the traits of a godly woman. The program culminates with the night of celebration where the father (or a father figure) reads a blessing that he has written and personalized for the young woman. He then places a crown on her head, declaring her a modern-day princess, a daughter of the King of kings. [3]

The Beginning: Beginning menses can be a traumatic experience. But a mother can turn trauma into triumph with a little tender loving care. Take her to get her first grown-up silky nightgown or a precious set of pearls. If she is older when she begins, have her makeup done at the department store makeup counter. Plan a special dinner at the fanciest café in town. Present her with a delicate charm bracelet that you can add to with every future big moment in her teen life. Somehow, some way, celebrate her beginning moment as a true woman.

Julie Hiramine, president of Generations of Virtue, wrote the Beautifully Made series to walk a girl through puberty. In the first book in the series, *Approaching Womanhood*, Julie explains how God is changing a girl's body and relays a positive message on menstruation. Julie says, "I try to celebrate with my girls when their period starts. I have found it a good idea to get prepared ahead of time by filling a gift bag with a selection of pads and items they will need when they begin their first period. I include the second book in the *Beautifully Made* series ([which] is designed to give to them when they start their period, with practical advice, and answers to common questions that every girl wants to know) and some fun little gift items that I know that particular girl would enjoy. Then I place the bag in the very top of my closet and wait for the day she comes to tell me her period has started." For an extra touch, Dad could bring his daughter flowers—a subtle, sweet celebration on a sensitive day.

Terrific Twelve. You might be able to beat your daughter to the starting line of womanhood by making her twelfth birthday a celebration packed with firsts. (For some early bloomers, you might need to move this up a year and do a "Double Digits" party at 11.) Buy her that first bra, a razor to shave her legs, her first set of high heels, or her first make-up set. You might take her to get her ears pierced. You choose whatever next step you feel is age-appropriate for your family. She might voice a desire for some form of activity to mark the movement into womanhood.

Once a Girl, Now a Woman: One family we know took their daughter on a weekend trip when she hit the "double digits." They flew to New York City and took her to the American Girl museum to get a doll made that looks just like her, making a memory of her appearance as a little girl. Then the next day, they went to shop for a grown-up outfit and went to a nice restaurant for dinner…and the next segment of "the talk" escorting her into womanhood.

For your daughter's Sweet 16, try one of these ideas to mark this big moment (or adapt it to whenever you feel she is ready to date):

On the Town: Host a formal dinner party where her closest friends (guys and gals) dress to the nines and eat the fanciest gourmet food you can afford. Play classical music—maybe you'll even go the extra mile and hire musicians!

Dance the Night Away: Host a dance where couples learn some classics, like the waltz, swing, tango, and two-step. You will have to spring for a band, dance instructor, and food, but it will definitely be a memory.

High Tea: Take your daughter and a few of her closest friends (and maybe their moms or all the female relatives) to high tea. Bring along photos of her growing-up years—and yours. Hand down a piece of jewelry that has been in the family for several generations.

Spiritual: Understanding God's Call

A tangible gift can be nice as you talk about the upcoming changes: a locket, a heart necklace, or a grown-up music or jewelry box for a girl or a cool tool like a Swiss army knife or a jersey with the number of his favorite Christian athlete (Tim Tebow's #15 comes to mind). However, no gift is as precious as your equipping your son or daughter for their future leadership role in society.

Your Son

When our youngest son was about to enter junior high, we presented him with a beautiful wooden box inscribed with a verse: "All these were...heads of families, choice men, brave warriors and outstanding leaders...men ready for battle" (1 Chronicles 7:40). We wished we had thought of this sooner and had given this to him on the day of the big reveal a few years earlier since we talked so much about what a privilege it is to be a father. We told our son that is why a man must be ready and prepared for the responsibility, working on his character all throughout his growing-up years so he is ready for this vital role and task God entrusts to men. (We also gave these boxes to our older sons that Christmas—we thought it was a good enough idea that we could make up for lost time!)

Each year on Father's Day we give each of our sons something to put in the box that will help them be a good dad someday: a Bible, a book, a CD, a tool, or a gadget. Now that our oldest son is a great father of three, he's putting all those gifts to good use!

A Man Ready

Look over 1 Chronicles 7:40 again. This verse contains vital information to share with your son. Why not plan a father-son getaway to do this a little later during puberty, maybe with one of the rites of passage listed above? Let's look at each role and you can best decide when to communicate this:

- *Heads of families:* "Head" means the beginning point, the brain, the source, the chief, or head leader. We need to prepare our sons to step up as leaders.

- *Choice men:* "Choice" here means pure or purified. We need to equip our sons to be moral leaders with integrity.

- *Brave warriors:* This can also be translated "mighty men of valor." We need to prepare our sons to be heroic, brave, courageous, and confident in the face of danger, threat, or the need to protect others. "Valor" means both physical strength and wealth. So we should also be equipping our sons to produce income and be good stewards of money, time, and physical fitness. (We thought of this verse when all of our sons wanted to spend so much time weight lifting!)

- *Outstanding leaders:* This means "head of princes or rulers." It is imperative to train sons to be comfortable leading other leaders and mentoring others to become leaders. Put your son in situations where he can meet and interact with people in charge of something and serving others in a variety of ways.

- *Men ready for battle:* Literally, this simply means they are prepared for war. (And could be interpreted as a positive command for military service.) But the "war" is on many fronts, so we also need to help our sons gain the ability to debate, stand up for their convictions and beliefs, and defend the truth.

Our friend Jack works for the sheriff's department. One day while pursuing a suspect, the perpetrator pulled a weapon and aimed it at Jack. His wife, upon hearing this terrifying story, asked, "So what did you do?"

Jack replied, "At that point you don't *get* ready, you *are* ready." Point well taken. We prepare well, we train, and we equip on the calm days so that we are all up for the battle when life smacks us in the face with a tough call or a split-second decision. That's your most important job as the parent of a boy: preparing him for the life-altering decisions and battles that are sure to come his way.

Your Daughter

Let's look at just two of the many Bible passages that can help pave the way for your daughter's noble role. In the first, I have added the meaning of key words into the passage in parentheses:

> Likewise, teach the older women to be reverent *(proper, religious, sacred)* in the way they live, not to be slanderers

(wicked or devilish) or addicted *(enslaved)* to much wine, but to teach what is good *(teaching what is right, beautiful, commendable)*. Then they can urge the younger women to love *(show friendship and kindness to)* their husbands and children, to be self-controlled *(moderate, prudent)* and pure *(holy)*, to be busy at home *(a home keeper, a heart for their home)*, to be kind *(moral, generous, good)*, and to be subject *(rank themselves under like a military officer)* to their husbands, so that no one will malign the word of God (Titus 2:3-5).

A girl is to be equipped to have a strong relationship with God, her future husband, her future children, her female mentors, and those who will experience the hospitality of her home and the kindness of her character. This is the place for showing that femininity can be modest, pure, and gentle.

> All the people of my town know that you are a woman of noble character (Ruth 3:11).

The word *noble* can be translated *woman of excellence, a woman who has strength of character, a woman of virtue, valiant, full of valor, strong,* or *mighty*. In Scripture the same word can also refer to a capable and elite army of powerful warriors.

Both young men and young women are encouraged to be servants of people *and* warriors for right. It is equally good and godly for a young woman to gain courage, confidence, bravery, and the willingness to go to battle for God's principles and protect the people on God's heart. Strong women attract strong men, so empower your girl to be bold for God.

As you talk with and train your daughter, helping her navigate the drastic body changes of puberty, you'll also have the perfect classroom to forge her people skills, her character, and her ability to gain the confidence and inner strength derived from a powerful connection to God.

By talking honestly and celebrating their transitions into the adult world, you build your relationship with your teen. Tweens and teens are drawn to adults who treat them like grown-ups.

So get ready, Mom and Dad, your child will be changing! And their change will also change your life. But the good news is that no matter how we as parents or our kids feel about the rolling tide of changes, the God who never changes is the Lord of infinity, and no change is out of His control.

Answers to Have Ready

You are definitely not alone in your pursuit to firmly establish wisdom in your child's life. Many organizations offer helpful tools and traditions. In addition to the ideas mentioned previously, here are a few more options to investigate:

Passport to Purity: Take your tween away for a special weekend with the parent of their gender. Using Family Life's "Passport to Purity" resource, discuss changing body issues and the new season of life that's coming. Add in an activity that reflects something your tween would like to do when he or she grows up. Help them picture the life they can live if they continue to make good choices during their teen years.

Suddenly They're 13: Dave and Claudia Arp describe a series of "Teenage Challenges" in their book *Suddenly They're 13*. Before his or her thirteenth birthday, the child is motivated to accomplish a series of challenging assignments, all of which teach vital life skills, in order to get a much desired reward. The idea of taking a year to prepare a child to cross into adult life is rooted in the Jewish heritage and the Bar Mitzvah celebration, as well as a few other cultures that take time to groom a youth for the responsibilities of adult life by giving them many of those experiences as they are tutored to success. Your family culture or heritage may also have a form of a rite of passage, and it is good to include or adapt these to your family. Building a bridge between generations serves your child well as they then have more people to go to if they hit a rough patch in the road of life.

Gift of Abstinence: The desire to help teens wait until marriage for sex cuts across culture, race, and party politics. In a 2012 study nearly eight out of ten Democrats and nine out of ten Republicans supported abstinence education.[4] It is because abstinence education is working: The Centers for Disease Control and Prevention reports that between 1988 and 2010, the number of sexually active girls between 15 and 19 dropped 8 percent. The number of boys who'd had sex dropped 18 percent![5] A study by the National Longitudinal Study of Adolescent Health reflected a lower likelihood of pregnancy for girls taking virginity pledges.[6] The True Love Waits ministry started helping teens make virginity pledges in 1993, and now a variety of ministries and organizations offer programs, pledges, and tokens to mark the commitment. The pledge reads, "I am making a commitment to myself, my family, and my Creator, that I will abstain from sexual activity of any kind before marriage. I will keep my body and my thoughts pure as I trust in God's perfect plan for my life." The card pledgers carry is inscribed with 1 Thessalonians 4:3-4: "It is God's will that you should be sanctified: that you should avoid sexual immorality; that each of you should learn to control your own body in a way that is holy and honorable."

Studies have since found a few factors help the pledge be more successful:

- if the teenager made the pledge from the heart instead of going along with the crowd
- if other peers have made the pledge and can provide support and accountability
- if parents are involved in supporting the pledge

It is also important for a teen to clearly realize that a virginity pledge should also include a commitment to avoid both oral and vaginal sex. These factors tell parents it is good to make the pledge both a private and a public experience, and that it is beneficial to have your tween and teen in youth ministries that will cooperate in reinforcing the values you hold dear in your family.

Many ministries—as well as your local Christian bookstore—offer purity rings. You can also create your own tangible reminder or gift. Later we will share what we did to help our sons make this vital choice.

Parent to Parent

One of the most brilliant parenting ideas we have heard of came from a set of small town parents. A mom had the brilliant idea of gathering all the parents in her church who had kids the same age. They began meeting the year the children were ready to enter first grade. The parents agreed to meet each year in August, right before school started, to talk through expected transitions and traditions for the coming school year. They tried for the most part to keep similar values and expectations on when certain privileges might be extended to their children. This way the kids couldn't use the "Everyone else is doing it!" line, because, well everyone else was *not* doing it! As the students entered the teen years, this group of parents all agreed to be the cool parents. They sponsored after-game gatherings and after-prom parties and were the chaperones for school and church functions.

While each family had their own methods for handling dating relationships, they decided as a group on a minimum age they would all stick to before allowing their children to date. They would attend conferences, planned father-son and mother-daughter trips, and rites of passage celebrations together. For the most part, because the parents became such great friends, the kids preferred to do things as a group too. They delayed dating naturally until later because they enjoyed being together as a group and didn't feel any pressure to single date.

As we lunched with several of the parents, we heard what their now-grown children had become: doctors, lawyers, educators, pastors—all with college educations, and many with master's and doctoral degrees. And all of them, each and every one of the kids, still had their faith intact and had lived a moral life of sexual integrity until marriage. They were Christian leaders and role models in their places of employment and communities. This meeting of the minds took a little effort each year, but it was well worth the time and energy because the fruit was so sweet!

Answers for Your Heart

This is the oasis time as a parent—a time to make precious memories with your child. Josh McDowell and Dick Day write, "Rules without relationship leads to rebellion; relationship without rules leads to confusion."[7] This is the season to build relationship with your child so as he or she goes into puberty and then their teen years, you will be seen as the strongest voice and the most powerful influencer (after God).

Later, when rules and guidelines are decided on, your relationship will have the strength to handle it—and your teen will desire to please you. Here is a worksheet to brainstorm some ways to build relationship with your child during the oasis season:

My child's favorite food:

My child's favorite color:

My child's favorite sport:

My child's favorite music or musician:

My child's favorite Bible character:

My child's favorite location in town to visit:

My child's favorite vacation spot:

My child's favorite member of the extended family:

My child's favorite dream day (something he/she has said he/she would like to do someday):

My child's favorite dessert:

My child's favorite role model:

My child's favorite activity at home:

My child's favorite friends:

My child's favorite spiritual activity or church activity:

Now look at the list of favorites and begin to brainstorm ideas to build a relationship with your child at age...

8 and 9:

10 and 11:

12 and 13:

Journal your feelings and prayers about your child leaving childhood and entering the teen years. How do you feel about all the changes ahead for your child and how they may affect you? Write down your feelings and then commit your requests to God in prayer, knowing He will be faithful to you and your child:

- To the faithful you show yourself faithful (Psalm 18:25).

- All the ways of the LORD are loving and faithful toward those who keep the demands of his covenant (Psalm 25:10).

- Send me your light and your faithful care, let them lead me; let them bring me to your holy mountain, to the place where you dwell (Psalm 43:3).

- For the LORD is good and his love endures forever; his faithfulness continues through all generations (Psalm 100:5).

What Is Gender and What Does It Mean to Me?

Strive for full restoration, encourage one another, be of one mind, live in peace. And the God of love and peace will be with you.

2 Corinthians 13:11

You are raising kids in a strenuous environment when it comes to the issue of gender identity. Politics, education, and entertainment have adopted sexual identity as a major point of discussion. As a result, concerned parents need to prepare themselves to answer sensitive and potentially embarrassing questions when it comes to their children's acceptance of their sexual identity.

The Mystery

Every child goes through a complex process of discovering the sexual reality of their life. It begins with an awareness of their body with all its wonder, physical capabilities, and ability to experience pleasure. It is impossible for young boys to not be aware that they have a penis or for young girls not to be aware they have a vagina. Since the head of the penis and the clitoris contain concentrated bundles of nerve endings, kids periodically experience sensations that feel good and get their attention.

The process of kids discovering the sexual realities of life can be awkward, humorous, and spontaneous. One couple was driving through central New Jersey when their eight-year-old daughter saw a road sign that read "Exit for Middlesex." She tapped her dad on the shoulder and asked, "Are there towns called Beginning Sex and Ending Sex?"[1]

The progression continues as emotional reactions take place in relationships. As kids grow, they meet people of both genders who touch their hearts. It is common for boys to become infatuated with girls in their peer group that create feelings in their heart, stomach, and groin that are strong and mysterious. It is also common for boys to be impressed by other boys in their peer group and conclude, "I want to be like them." In the same way, girls become infatuated with boys and meet girls in their peer group who elicit strong emotional reactions. These emotional responses are captivating, mysterious, and too powerful to ignore, so they become part of the process of determining a young person's gender identity.

Adolescence adds another layer of complexity as hormones create dramatic changes in the bodies of young men and women and relationships become a major factor in their lives. Teens experience such dramatic change that their orientation to life actually takes a different course than it did when they were kids and the course it will take as adults. In simplest terms, teens experiment with their lives. The dramatic development of their bodies and the vibrant nature of their emotions make it harder for them to think through the issues of life and develop discernment. The typical approach is for teens to move from peer group to peer group trying on different identities. When they are with athletes, they take on an athletic approach to life. When they are with musicians, they act like musicians. When they are with the technologically competent, they build their lives around technology. When they are with the socially popular, they play the game with skill, and so on. They can literally be different people in the morning, at lunch, during the afternoon, and then at home, all in one day.

When it comes to sorting out the issues of their heart, they tend to "feel" their way through. If they are romantically attached to a member of the opposite sex, they think, "This is great. We are so close and my feelings for this person are so strong. It must be love." If they notice that someone of the same sex is attractive, they may think, "Why am I attracted to this person? What does this say about me? Does this mean I am homosexual or bisexual?" If no one seems to pay attention to them, they may conclude, "Something must be wrong with me. If I was normal, I would be asked out on a date. I have never had a boyfriend/girlfriend so I must not be attractive."

As adults, we tend to overreact to these developmental steps in our kids' lives by either accusing them of being perverted or homosexual or by not addressing their behavior at all. Stan and Brenna Jones share insight that all parents ought to keep in mind as they help their kids navigate these emotionally charged waters:

> Because teenage sexual arousal can be unfocused, many normal heterosexual teens find themselves on occasion feeling sexual response to hearing about homosexual acts or thinking about another girl's or boy's body. Help teenagers to take this in stride by recognizing it for what it is. They are going through a period when identity as a sexual mature adult is being shaped...Only 11 percent of young men who initially reported they had some same sex attraction still reported those feelings a year later. Earlier in this process they do not have a definite "form" to their sexuality as they will later. Warn them about these experiences, and tell them not to worry about them. Such occasional feelings are to be expected and will eventually resolve. Their job during this period is to be thankful for their awakening sexual feelings, make the right decisions God wishes for them, enjoy their relationships, and be patient with themselves as they grow up. They do not have to act on any of the sexual feelings they experience.
>
> Children and teenagers engage in sexual experimentation, including same-sex behavior, and this needs to be discussed as well...Same sex experimentation can take the forms of guys wrestling and grabbing each other's genitals, girls practicing kissing or petting as they talk about dating, two boys watching each other masturbate, and so forth. It is vital not to label such behavior as homosexual; to do so is to brand the person on the basis of an action. If

you discover your child engaging in any of these activities, never say, "Stop that homosexual play!" or "Are you trying to be gay?" Children can be branded by such statements. Instead discipline them for their failures to protect the privacy and sanctity of their own bodies, but always in the context of affirming their normalcy.[2]

Steer the Power

Gender influence and sexual attraction is one of the most powerful forces in the lives of our kids. The desire, curiosity, and temptations that accompany sexual development are emotionally and chemically powerful even though they lack the ability to think and discern. They have been given by God to create motivation to be in relationship with another caring, committed individual and to give rise to the next generation. Beyond that, our sexual urges do not, on their own, think through long-term implications or discern the emotional, spiritual, or interpersonal health of those we are attracted to.

For boys, we like to compare our sexual drive to fast, powerful automobiles. I (Bill) had the opportunity to travel 130 miles per hour in a Mini Cooper on Germany's autobahn. It was an awesome experience that was made even more awesome by the presence of a Porsche Turbo. I first saw it in the rearview mirror as it appeared to stalk us like prey. We moved over to the right lane as the Porsche blew by us as if we were standing still. I may be mistaken but I think the powerful engine growled at us when it passed by. I remember thinking, "Wow, I wish I could be in the driver's seat of that car!"

Within an hour we passed the same car, except this time it didn't look like a car. It was a crumpled, smashed clump of metal. The driver of the car failed to have proper respect for the power of the machine he was driving. He skidded out of control, smashed into a concrete pillar, and ended the experience with extreme damage. It's not hard to see the parallel with the sexual reality of our lives. The power is awesome, but it needs to be controlled and guided by sound thinking and clear decisions.

Most girls are not as impressed with powerful machines but they can be equally captivated by friendships and clothing. Young ladies seem to implicitly understand the power of interaction. They love conversations, friendship activities, fitting in, being loved, and finding acceptance among their peers. One woman we know describes relationships as "the jet fuel that empowers their lives." Girls are right in identifying the potential of relationships, but that doesn't mean that every relationship is safe or desirable. Friends must be chosen wisely with discernment or they can create turmoil, ruin reputations, and distract responsible young people from their real priorities. The draw to friendship is powerful, but it must be directed by sound thinking and healthy decisions.

Clothing likewise can become an overstated issue in the life of a young lady. One of our granddaughters had the opportunity to attend a parent/child soccer seminar. The plan for the day was to have both parent and child on the field learning soccer skills to introduce young kids to the game. Well, the day came and our little angel insisted on wearing a princess dress complete with high heels and a crown to the soccer practice. She was cute but her clothing did not fit the context. In the same way, romantic and sexual desires are strong and attractive but they have a context that must be guarded with wisdom and resolve.

We never want to tell our kids and teens that their sexual feelings are wrong because they have been given by God for good and to add value to our lives. At the same time, we never want to naïvely accept the notion that all sexual decisions are of equal value or think our kids will figure out the context and boundaries on their own. Just as we give young people driving lessons and take young ladies shopping to help them learn these pursuits with skill, we want to help them develop skills that lead them to a healthy acceptance of their gender and all the wonders that go along with the way God created them.

In helping our young people reach biblical conclusions about their gender, we must keep in mind that they are living in a minefield. It has become fashionable in politics, education, and entertainment to glamorize and legitimize homosexual relationships. Since these influences confront them every day, it can be rather intimidating to the young people we care so deeply about. In addition, the conversation that is taking place in the public arena is based on emotional, self-centered conclusions rather than logic. Our kids are being told they are mean-spirited or have a hateful attitude if they disagree with the emotional conclusions being presented to them. In light of this, we as loving parents must speak the truth with simplicity, conviction, compassion, and heartfelt passion.

Boys and Girls Are Different

We have written extensively on the topic of gender in our book *Men Are Like Waffles—Women Are Like Spaghetti*. We *know* that boys and girls are different! It all begins with creation. The Bible clearly states, "So God created mankind in his own image, in the image of God he created them; male and female he created them" (Genesis 1:27). Every boy and every girl is a reflection of the image of God. We love because God loves. We are creative because God is creative. We are passionate about life because God is passionate about life. In His creative genius, God chose to reflect His image in two different genders. Both are equally valuable, equally beautiful in design, equally capable of significant influence, and equally filled with awe and wonder. When we accept and exalt the differences, we honor God as the Creator of life.

We also line up our minds and hearts with reality since research increasingly validates the fact that men and women are different by design. Of course, there are obvious physical differences that can be seen with even the most cursory glance. There are, in addition, profound differences between males and females that cannot be seen with the naked eye. Here are some of the more interesting differences:

When a man solves problems he uses only one side of his brain. A woman uses both sides of her brain when solving a problem. While every fetus begins its path in life as a female, the presence of the Y chromosome in males sends out a signal to interrupt the development in the female direction with high levels of testosterone. During this "testosterone bath," many of the connections between the two sides of the brain are severed. As a result, women literally have more connections between the two sides of their brains than men.

When a man eats, the part of his brain that makes him feel happier is stimulated. When a woman eats, the part of her brain that sharpens her eyesight is stimulated. She becomes more aware of her environment and has more to talk about. This is the reason so many good memories are developed around meals. One of the best ways to build healthy relationships is to deliberately and consistently share meals with the people you love.

Men seek out risk and danger more often than women. This happens because males have higher levels of testosterone in their bodies than females, which influences a more aggressive approach to life. "Women appear to be less willing to risk being caught and convicted of speeding than men…On average women made safer choices than men when it came to making risky consumer decisions, such as smoking behavior, seat-belt use, preventative dental care, and having regular blood pressure checks."[3]

While male brains are, on average, ten percent larger than female brains, the part of the brain that monitors verbal fluency is larger in females. As a result, boys learn to influence through rough play while girls learn to influence through words. "Young boys come to appreciate a power that resides in an active, physical world; and later, as men, they rely more on physical withdrawal as one means of coping with challenges. But women (vs. men) rely more on language—verbal and nonverbal—to influence others, to the extent that as young girls they polish their communicative skills in managing personal problems. Accordingly, women tend to use a wider array of communication strategies, including negative messages, when confronting their partners."[4]

This reinforces the observation that young ladies are more active in relationships than young men. They tend to have more friends, experience more self-disclosure and intimacy in their friendships, and exhibit similar behavior with both male and female friends. Young men, on the other hand, tend to limit the number of friends they have and change their behavior around girls to be less combative, competitive, and aggressive. As a result, a boy is often under more stress when he interacts with a girl and a girl gets disappointed more often as she tries to figure out why the boy she likes is awkward around her.

Marriage Is a Major Part of Our Value System

As believers in Christ, we understand that the relationship between a husband and wife is the clearest picture of God's saving grace on earth. "For this reason a man will leave his father and mother and be united to his wife, and the two will become one flesh. This is a profound mystery—but I am talking about Christ and the church" (Ephesians 5:31-32). It is a spiritual value we hold dear because it helps proclaim the greatest message in the world. God created us and wants to have a relationship with each and every one of us. To make it possible, Jesus died on the cross for our shortcomings so He can offer forgiveness freely. God loves us unconditionally and He asks us to respect Him, honor Him, and follow Him. To help us understand how a relationship with Him works, He gave us the relationship between a husband who loves his wife and a wife who respects her husband.

We do not, however, live in a society where everyone is a Christian. What, then, are the values that guide our laws and decisions as a society? This is where the Judeo-Christian ethic comes into play. It is a worldview that assigns the values upon which our society operates. These values provide stability, wisdom, and direction when it comes to the decisions that shape society and limit people's activities. In America, we invest in education because we hold the value that all citizens ought to be educated. We punish those who commit murder because we value human life. We prosecute financial fraud because we value personal ownership of property and contractual integrity. The same value system that gives us our most cherished rights and privileges includes a conviction that marriage is a relationship between a man and a woman. Redefining marriage would require that we adopt a different value system than the one America was built upon and gave people the freedom to even talk about changing it.

Our values also respect people's right to choose lifestyles we may not personally endorse. We are not on a crusade to persecute or aggressively hinder people from having relationships we disagree with. Our value system, however, does not include these relationships in the definition of marriage. It is interesting that this one type of relationship has been singled out for redefinition. We willingly say that each of us can only have one spouse so we do not refer to polygamy as marriage. We cannot marry when we are minors and we cannot marry people to whom we are too closely related. Few of us would ever feel pressure to change the definition of marriage in these cases or be made to believe we are hateful and judgmental if we refuse to do so. That is because these relationships are defined by a value system we collectively trust. Helping our kids hold to the historical view of marriage is, therefore, training them to trust the values that build the most successful societies.

Gender Is Genetic

When we talk about being male and female we are talking about a reality of life that can be genetically verified. A female has two X chromosomes that affect the development of every cell in her body. A male has one X chromosome and one Y chromosome that likewise affect the development of every cell in his body. These chromosomes are carried in every cell of the human body so a test of any would verify the individual as either male or female.

It should be noted that most of the differences between males and females are related to hormones. Men's muscles are larger; women's hips are wider. Men grow facial hair; women do not. Women's lungs are more efficient when it comes to metabolizing oxygen; men break down lactic acid more efficiently so they experience less cramping. The list goes on because there is a genetic foundation. The Y chromosome contains a sex-determining gene called SRY which stands for "Sex-determining Region of the Y chromosome." The SRY gene converts the gonad cells of the early human embryo into testes, which in turn triggers development of male sexual organs. This leads to a testosterone bath in the womb and the production of high levels of testosterone during puberty that creates profound differences between the genders.

Homosexuality Is a Choice

Homosexuals will often say, "I was born like this. I have always been this way." Homosexuality is now being wrongly labeled as a civil rights issue, just like race and gender. This is unfortunate because homosexuality cannot be objectively confirmed. It is a self-reported condition that has no genetic, scientific, or physical means to evaluate whether the claims made by the individual are true or not.

Different groups have varying opinions about the morality and appropriateness of the homosexual lifestyle and it is healthy for us as a society to give all parties an opportunity to share their opinions. Taking a self-reported personal choice, however, and elevating it to the status of a civil right blurs the discussion and establishes a purely emotional basis for discriminating against the majority of the population. We would never accept this line of thinking for other areas of life. For instance, if someone vehemently proclaimed that he had blue skin when he obviously did not, we wouldn't accept it as true. And yet for some reason we are being told that homosexuality is different from all other choices in life.

As concerned parents, we must hold the line on the facts. We understand this is a lifestyle choice even though the current of modern culture is attempting to say otherwise. Our kids are going to hear emotional appeals and friendly demands that they accept the legitimacy of the homosexual lifestyle. We can't combat the assault with simple logic. We must have calm conviction based on truth. If we get intimidated by the assertions, appear to be afraid of the conversation, overreact to the statements our kids repeat, or respond with anger when the topic is brought up, our kids will assume what they heard outside our home is true. If, however, we are confident in our position, consistent in our assertions, open to answering questions for which we know the answers, and committed to finding answers to new questions, our kids are likely to conclude that we know what we're talking about.

Homosexuality Is Rare

If you base your conclusions on what you hear from modern culture, you would think that homosexuality is pervasive and commonplace. In a 2011 Gallup poll Americans estimated that 25 percent of the population was homosexual.[5] The next year, Gallup conducted another poll in which 121,290 people responded to the question, "Do you, personally, identify as lesbian, gay, bisexual, or transgender?" The result of this survey was that only 3.4 percent of the population actually identify themselves according to one of these titles.[6] In light of this, we must communicate the rarity of these alternative lifestyles confidently and consistently without overreacting.

Regardless, 80 percent of homosexual men and 70 percent of homosexual women report having been sexually abused. If your child is expressing gender concern issues, there might be more pain under the surface. Getting qualified counseling is certainly in order.

Homosexuality Is Not the Ultimate Sin

In an attempt to protect our children, we often react to discussions about homosexuality with disdain, disgust, and demeaning remarks. This is usually well-intentioned, but it is neither necessary nor appropriate and has the potential to backfire. If we overreact to the conversations about alternative lifestyles, we run the risk of encouraging undue curiosity, eliciting intense reactions that overshadow logic, or creating a reputation for being judgmental and unapproachable. If these responses take hold, our kids will avoid us as they make decisions about their sexual activity rather than consulting us.

We live in a world where some people will quickly accuse us of hating those who choose an alternative lifestyle simply because we disagree with them. We cannot stop them from jumping to that conclusion, but we can keep them from confirming their thinking by remaining loving, compassionate, and conversational. Our kids will pay attention to our approach and they will evaluate what they hear as they interact with their peers. Rest assured: Calm confidence on our part is a powerful counterbalance to emotional leverage when it comes to our own children.

The human race has a history of responding poorly to behavior that is explicitly restricted. It began in the Garden of Eden when God said to Adam, "You must not eat from the tree of the knowledge of good and evil, for when you eat from it you will certainly die" (Genesis 2:17). Satan played upon people's natural curiosity when he tempted Eve to break that one rule.

Ever since, men and women have been captivated by this same process. We begin to wonder why we "must not" do this or that. We evaluate what God has said about the way life works the best. Curiosity and the desire to be in relationship with others breaks down our willingness to exercise self-control. The notion that a forbidden behavior actually makes you more insightful, more enlightened, and more modern takes over. The Old Testament and human history have proven that this approach does not lead to healthy decisions.

Excellence Is the Goal of Grace

In contrast, the grace of the New Testament presents a pursuit of excellence based on who we are. The attitude of the New Testament is you have been created by God, chosen by God, and adopted into God's own family. You are the place on earth where the Holy Spirit dwells. As such, it makes sense that you would live a life of excellence, pursuing worthwhile goals and self-discipline. Athletes work out extensively and monitor their diets because they want to compete effectively. Musicians practice relentlessly and avoid activities that would interrupt their ability to play the music they love. In the same way, we will seek to make high-quality decisions and pursue healthy relationships when we embrace the reality of who we are in Christ.

As parents, we will be most effective when we consistently remind our kids they are valuable, talented, capable, and worthy of honor. It is easy for us to be afraid for our kids because of the challenges in our world and to resort to constant criticism and intense reactions in an effort to keep them safe. In parenting by fear, however, you run the risk of tapping into that unhealthy curiosity that has plagued the human race. How many young people have concluded, "Well, my mom and dad already think I am bad and will mess up so I might as well do it." Instead, we want to be instruments of grace who lovingly correct poor behavior as we train our kids and applaud their successes. When it comes to gender identity specifically, we want to affirm over and over that our gender is God's creative plan and that He made us either male or female because He knows it is best for us.

Answers to Have Ready

We cannot leave this decision to the impulses and experiences of our kids. Sexual decisions are some of the most important choices in the lives of our children. First Corinthians 6:18-20 states, "Flee from sexual immorality. All other sins a person commits are outside the body, but whoever sins sexually, sins against their own body. Do you not know that your bodies are temples of the Holy Spirit, who is in you, whom you have received from God? You are not your own; you were bought at a price. Therefore honor God with your bodies." Sexual immorality includes sex before marriage, sex after marriage with someone who is not a spouse, pornography, homosexuality, and any other activities that involve sexual arousal with anyone to whom you are not married.

If your child is struggling with a gender identity issue, do exactly what you would do if he or she had any illness or emotional pain. Find the best experts, the best doctors, and the best mentors and create a team of support, safety, and biblically sound advice to guide you and your child through the rough waters to the stable shore.

As parents, our desire is to protect the hearts of our kids and to enable them to experience the full influence of the Holy Spirit. Every sexual choice affects the condition of their hearts and their comfort level with the presence of the Holy Spirit in their lives. As your son or daughter is in tune with God, God will layer gender identity confirmations into his or her life in small ways, day upon day, until they are secure in their gender identification. Our job is just to echo the truth about what God says about men and women and allow it to sink into the soil of our child's heart and mind.

Despite what you may have heard, your influence as parents still has a more profound effect on your kids than the media, peers, or any other adults in their lives. As you confidently remind your children that they are created in the image of God and are highly valued, you can anticipate that they will hold to God's values in their ever-shifting world.

Parent to Parent

You will need to have a few sentences ready to talk with friends and family about this very prominent topic. The National Organization for Marriage explains the best wording to explain a pro traditional marriage view is simply: "Gays and lesbians have a right to live as they choose, they don't have the right to redefine marriage for all of us."[7]

In 1 Corinthians 6:9-11 the apostle Paul clearly explains that God's will is that we choose to leave behind behaviors that God does not see as healthy for our lives:

> Or do you not know that wrongdoers will not inherit the kingdom of God? Do not be deceived: Neither the sexually immoral nor idolaters nor adulterers nor men who have sex with men nor thieves nor the greedy nor drunkards nor slanderers nor swindlers will inherit the kingdom of God. And that is what some of you were. But you were washed, you were sanctified, you were justified in the name of the Lord Jesus Christ and in the Spirit of our God.

There are two important things to note in this verse. First, homosexuality is in a list of many sins and not singled out as any worse than the heterosexual sin of fornication or others named. Second, these sins are listed in the past tense—"This is what some of you *were*." This clearly teaches that you cannot be a Christ follower and follow your own lust for the same sex. It is a choice that must be made—"God's view or my own view." We encourage you to help your child, tween, or teen to elect for God's view on all topics, including this one.

You should be equipped to answer questions and defend your views on traditional marriage, homosexuality, bisexuality, and any other form of sexuality outside God's intended plan of one man and one woman for life.

Answers for Your Heart

Dakota Ary was a freshman football player and honor student at his public school. A teacher posted a photo of two men kissing. Disturbed by it, he told his parents and together they again talked through what the Bible says about homosexuality. Shortly after this, the teacher brought up the subject of homosexuality in class and a student, one of Dakota's friends, asked what Christianity had to say about the subject. Dakota turned to address his friend and he shared his thoughts, saying that he believed the Bible and God thought homosexuality was wrong. The teacher suspended Dakota and he was sent to a four-hour in-school suspension room, missing some of his other classes. With help from the Liberty Counsel, Dakota and his family filed suit against the school and teacher for taking away his right to free speech. Dakota's mom said, "Parents need to empower their children [and show them] that they are going to back them up." They won the suit. [8]

So perhaps there needs to be a new game show. Instead of "Are You Smarter Than a Fifth Grader?" it should be "Are You Braver Than a Freshman?"

When our oldest son was a freshman we daily encouraged him to stand up for his beliefs and God's values. One day in a quiet time God simply asked, "Are you being as brave as you are asking your son to be?" That day became the seed for the book *Becoming a Brave New Woman*. In that book I (Pam) wrote, "Show me the size of your God and I'll show you the size of your courage. Big God—Big Courage."

Write down a list of your fears, and then write down one of God's traits that will counteract those fears (compassionate, forgiving, righteous, loving, etc.). Look up some verses about that trait and begin to memorize and meditate on those verses to bolster your courage. That way you'll have plenty of courage to loan to your kids as they need it! My job is to know God, and the natural outcome is God will make me brave. Your job is to know God so He will make you brave. And if we help our kids know God, He will make them brave too.

Will You Help Me Avoid Mistakes?

And this is my prayer: that your love may abound more and more
in knowledge and depth of insight, so that you may be able
to discern what is best and may be pure and blameless.

Philippians 1:9-10

Some days the contrasts are sharp and obvious. Bill and I were recently headed to a pro-life fund-raiser for a local crisis pregnancy center. We were going to listen to Pam Tebow, and I was excited to hear her mommy wisdom. She raised five amazing kids, including the famed Heisman trophy winner Tim Tebow. Bill was the emcee for the evening. We parked in the far parking lot and crossed along the sidewalk that divided the local city park from the Arts Center where our event would take place. The beautiful San Diego sun was setting. It had been a warm afternoon and several teenage couples were scattered around the park. A few were kissing. The youth pastor and mom in me wanted to take action to help them all make better choices, but God drew my heart to one couple on the far side of the park.

This couple was much further along in their foreplay. He was on top of his "date" and her legs were spread open. He was in the rhythm of coitus, pants on but riding low. Honestly, I was pretty sure we were about ready to witness a premarital teenage "crisis pregnancy" in the making. My heart flooded with all the statistics, all the pages and pages of negative consequences I knew from my years in ministry and the research for this book. I could not just pass by, so I ran across the park in my high heels and black cocktail dress. A few feet from them, I began to realize where I was—in a park known for its gang activity. People had been shot and stabbed on the lawn into which my heels were now sinking. As I got closer, I thought that perhaps this young man could also be a part of a local gang. Nonetheless, he was someone's son and moreover, the teenage girl was someone's daughter. He was not respecting himself and he was definitely not respecting her—and this disrespect for intimacy and commitment was on display for all the public park to see.

In my passion to protect, that mama inside just took over. As I got nearer I began to talk loudly enough to give him the opportunity to make a better choice. I tried to convince them both to make a different choice. As I wrapped up, I leaned in and said, "But most of all, this just isn't a good choice for either of you. God has a better plan for you." The young woman nodded in agreement and gave a thumbs-up sign as if to say, "I hear ya, lady." She pushed her date off her and he rolled away in a huff, shouting that his behavior wasn't against the law.

I don't know if that encounter will change anything in their future. They might have felt this old lady was all "up in their business," but for that moment in time, maybe my interruption delayed a crisis and perhaps provided one more opportunity to rethink their choices. I pray so, or they will soon need the services of the crisis pregnancy center we raised funds for!

Many adults have simply thrown in the towel, concluding, "All teens will have sex, so why fight it?" But when is conceding defeat ever a good choice? Do we just give up the fight against terrorism, drinking and driving, genocide, rape, illegal drugs, or any other part of society's malaise? No, we press on. We can turn things around: If we all care, if we all speak up, if we all seek to educate, support, and encourage the teens of this generation, things can change. God cheers us on in this worthy battle. "Let us not become weary in doing good, for at the proper time we will reap a harvest if we do not give up" (Galatians 6:9).

But we have to be watchmen—on many fronts—on many

walls—as our kids enter the tween and teen years. It's like our kids are walking in a minefield, with explosives ready to blow up at their every step. Our kids are asking us to help them avoid the land mines. They may not verbally ask for help, but they have some legitimate fears as they look ahead at the teen landscape too. They're asking for help with choices about media, friends, urges, and mistakes.

One of our friends is an explosive device technician (an expert at defusing bombs) for the military. He went to a specialized school to be trained in how to safely neutralize the danger. To be successful at this risky task, he must fully understand the enemy and the enemy's weapons. It is the same with our task as parents. We are the trainers and our teens are the ones who must be fully equipped to successfully defuse the land mines. Our goal is to help push the enemy further and further back so more prisoners of this war on values can be freed. Let's look at the arsenal and how to equip our kids to counteract the attack.

Media

Media is forging an all-out war against our Christian family value system. My friend Julie Hiramine, founder of *Generations of Virtue*, writes about media, peer pressure, and eroding sexual values in her new book, *Guardians of Purity*. I won't repeat all her good advice, but I will point out a few important statistics to whet your appetite for this helpful resource:

- The average child spends more than 53 hours a week engaging with media (more than an adult will spend at work).

- 71 percent of teens have a TV in their own room (as well as 43 percent of those ages four to six and 30 percent of those under three).

- 90 percent of kids ages eight to sixteen have viewed porn online (67 percent of boys and 49 percent of girls saw nothing wrong with doing it).

- Only three out of ten teenagers have any rules overseeing their media use.[1]

We created a media contract as a way to help your tweens and teens think through their media choices. This can include reading (on websites or e-readers), television, radio (online or traditional), internet use, gaming, movies, cell phones, social media, and video use. We also encourage you to download a free copy of "The Beatitudes of Social Media" article at our website (www.love-wise.com). A side benefit of the media contract is it can help prevent your child from becoming the victim of an online predator because he or she will learn to be a safe, savvy, street-smart internet user. We, of course, recommend internet filters, television parental control settings, and all the software safeguards that technology can provide. (There is even a DVD player called Clearplay that will take any movie and edit it as it plays to make it G-rated!) However, there is no substitute for discernment, inner conviction, and a resolve for righteousness. In his book *Moral Revolution*, Kris Vallotton says:

> Your virtues train your attitudes, attitudes dictate your choices, choices decide your behavior, and your behavior determines your destiny. The way that this whole process begins is by giving your virtues authority over your thoughts. If your virtues do not govern what you allow yourself to think about, this process of reaching your destiny will be sabotaged. Trying to behave inside your virtues, without taking control of what movie is being shown in the theater room of your heart, simply won't work. Everything in life begins with a thought, an image that is projected on the movie screen of your mind.[2]

Media feeds thoughts and the virtues (or lack thereof) into your teen's life, so regulating media intake should be a priority while parenting a tween or teen. On our website we offer a Teen Media Contract that you can download to help your teens think through the major decisions having to do with all forms of media and technology use. We recommend that you have your child complete the contract, sign the pledge to media purity, and then reward him or her with movie tickets or a gift card to download music or a video, thus rewarding his or her newfound discernment.

The main principle of the media contract is to build that inner compass that will help a person make wise choices when no one is around but God. Remind your child of Philippians 4:8: "Finally, brothers and sisters, whatever is true, whatever is noble, whatever is right, whatever is pure, whatever is lovely, whatever is admirable—if anything is excellent or praiseworthy—think about such things." One family we know taped these verses to the TV and the remote control as a reminder of what to watch. If this is what a person takes in throughout his or her life, they will gain the ability to produce great literature and award-winning media. We can help develop the Christian community to inspire the world and take back the hearts and minds of our society, moving us all closer to the plan God intended.

Jesus said, "You will know them by their fruits...So every good tree bears good fruit, but the bad tree bears bad fruit" (Matthew 7:16-17 NASB). He went on to explain that "the things that proceed out of the mouth come from the heart, and those defile the man. For out of the heart come evil thoughts, murders, adulteries, fornications, thefts, false witness, slanders" (Matthew 15:18-19 NASB). This is the basic "Garbage in, garbage out" principle. What goes into a heart, mind, and soul is the kind of fruit that will be produced. If nothing edifying is what is digested, it is almost guaranteed you will see a life in a downward spiral. However, if you raise the quality of the morality and excellence of what is put into a life, that child will soar!

Here is a simple pledge that we suggest you *and* your teen sign. The best kind of leadership is by example!

> I commit to guard my heart, my ears, my mind, and my spirit by selecting excellence in what I read, watch, and listen to. I will be honest to my accountability partners and parents when asked what I am inputting into my soul, and I will seek to glorify God in all ways, at all times, in all things. I will hold to a standard of integrity using the same media in public and in private. I commit to all this before God with my whole heart.
>
> Signed:
> Date:

My Friends

The peer group makes all the difference at this stage of life. The best strategy to help a child make good peer choices is to raise them with a balance of compassion and righteousness. Compassion keeps them reaching out and their peers will look to your child as a leader and example. Help your child see the honor and the responsibility that comes with leadership. The below passage lists the qualities of an overseer, and it's a good set of goals to prepare our teens to emulate. (While this text is in the context of men who lead a church, the list is a nice set of character qualities that will serve both genders in any form of leadership well.)

> An elder must be blameless, faithful to his wife, a man whose children believe and are not open to the charge of being wild and disobedient. Since an overseer manages God's household, he must be blameless—not overbearing, not quick-tempered, not given to drunkenness, not violent, not pursuing dishonest gain. Rather, he must be hospitable, one who loves what is good, who is self-controlled, upright, holy and disciplined. He must hold firmly to the trustworthy message as it has been taught, so that he can encourage others by sound doctrine and refute those who oppose it (Titus 1:6-9).

In addition, teach your teen to walk in step with God's Holy Spirit. Here's a simple way to explain being in step with God's Spirit that we learned from Dr. Bill Bright of Campus Crusade for Christ (now Cru). When we were in youth ministry, I (Pam) often used a set of salt and pepper shakers to explain this.

You are the pepper and you are walking with the salt (God). You are meant to be a matching set, staying next to each other. As you go through life, God might whisper to your heart, *Say this, do that.* Often He will do this as you read the Bible, but we should learn to tune our ears to God's Spirit all day every day. He will also point out sin. That's when you have a choice. You can do what the Bible says in 1 John 1:9 and "confess [your] sins," believing that God is faithful to forgive. Or you can argue about the sin, and your heart and life begin to wander away from God. At first it might seem fun or enjoyable, but soon you might think things like, "Why am I so miserable? Why isn't my life fulfilling or running smoothly? Why do I feel far from God?" Your goal is to equip your child to stay in step, obeying at the first moment God whispers to his or her heart so they can stay in the center of God's plan for their life.

One way to help a tween or teen make wise friendship choices is to help him or her gain a wide net of friends in many settings and circles. By having a wide net of friends, if one group begins to wander from God your child will have other (wiser) friends to fellowship and socialize with. To achieve this, we encouraged our sons to be involved in many Christian youth groups and parachurch groups. We made it a tradition for our teens to attend our church on Sunday (as we served as a family there) but we were open to them visiting other youth groups during the week. They were also involved in Christian clubs, such as Fellowship of Christian Athletes, Teen Impact, and Student Venture. In some cities, in addition to these, Youth for Christ or other Christian groups might be options. Sit down with your teen and lay out all the options. Have them develop a multifaceted plan for developing strong Christian friendships.

Our own sons all went to Christian schools through eighth grade. The older two wanted to be missionaries on their local public high school campus as athletes, but by the time our youngest arrived on the scene, he was very discouraged by the darkness and eroding education there. At this point Bill had the opportunity to change jobs and move cities, so Caleb attended a very strong Christian high school.

It is interesting though, that the sons in public school and the one in Christian school all had many social circles of Christian friends and pre-believing friends who followed our sons' leadership. However, they all needed to make strategic choices at times to change friendship circles when they were unable to persuade some of the friends to follow God's will for their lives.

In a baccalaureate address, our son Zach once advised high school graduates, "If you can't change your friends then change your friends." If your kids can't sway their friends to righteousness, they need to move themselves to fellowship with others who are seeking God's will. Peer pressure is a powerful thing—and it can work for your family. If your kids surround themselves with others who also want to make smart choices, it will be easier for them to keep choosing well.

My Urges

We've already discussed how to help teens handle feelings for the same gender, and in the next chapter we will discuss how to help a teen "pre-decide" how to handle feelings and actions within a dating relationship. But right now we'll focus on how to help teens handle urges that might be leading them to self-stimulation (masturbation). This is the topic parents usually want to pretend doesn't exist. But it does exist, and your teen needs you to be brave and discuss it.

The main reason to address masturbation is that if it is left unaddressed it can escalate, becoming addictive and depriving your son or daughter of the interpersonal relationships that lead to healthy dating and a healthy marriage. If they enter marriage addicted to masturbation, especially if it is linked to an addiction to pornography, it will erode the sex life God intended. The second reason is that excessive masturbation can lower a teen's inhibitions. They become used to a sexual release and then in a dating relationship, they will want that same sexual release. Lastly, if sex is created for marriage, that implies it is made for a relationship of two. If only one person is involved, it is being used outside its intended purpose.

Masturbation and porn addictions often go hand in hand. In either case, it is your responsibility to help your son or daughter regain control over his or her urges, desires, and passions. In general, try to avoid shaming or outrageous statements like, "If you do that you'll go blind" or the simplistic suggestions to "Take a cold shower" or "Think of your grandmother" if an urge hits. These threats might work, but a realistic plan for success will work better. The Bible doesn't directly talk about masturbation, so let's look at some principles that will help your son or daughter not be mastered by masturbation or become a prisoner of porn. Here is a list of what a teen should keep in his or her life and what needs to be removed.

First, *keep sexual feelings but remove igniters.* God created sexual feelings, but when those feelings are put in the driver's seat they can escalate into masturbation and porn addictions. Some factors act like accelerants to the addictions, and it's your job to help your teen rid himself of:

- sexually saturated media of all kinds
- leisurely nakedness (lounging around with little or nothing on)
- long lengths of time alone, especially in his or her room with the door shut
- unregulated internet access
- dating boundary violations (making out, petting in or outside of clothing, mutual masturbation, etc.)

All of these things can be fuel to sexual desires. If you can set up preventions within your home early, they will be easier to reinforce later. These can be simple things like having a computer in a main family room, doing homework with the door to their room open, or leaving a door open unless you're changing clothes. An open-door home is an invitation to integrity.

In our home, those of the opposite sex were not allowed in bedrooms, even with the door open, and if our teens had friends in, we tried our best to always have a parent on site. Those of the opposite gender were never allowed inside to visit if we weren't home, and our sons were instructed to follow this rule at others' homes as well as our own.

Second, *keep guilt but remove shame.* We would never recommend that your teen take the boundaries off and masturbate any time, but we also do not encourage them to wallow in shame. Responsive guilt that motivates us to repent from poor decisions is a good thing, but chronic shame can become a destructive force that causes people to become self-absorbed, self-centered, and self-destructive. Jesus died to free us from our shame, and He calls us to walk in grace. When we regularly dwell on our shame rather than confessing our sins and accepting

God's forgiveness, we fight against the growth He is trying to accomplish in us. The goal is to stay focused on God's grace. Godly guilt realigns our path, correcting our choices to keep us nearer the heart of God; shame causes us to run from the heart and presence of God.

Third, *keep self-control but remove compulsions.* Pornography, masturbation, and other behaviors attached to sexuality can become a powerful habitual addiction. Other more important priorities like studies, work, friendships, or their relationship with God can go by the wayside as compulsions are fed. Help your child learn to be self-controlled in all areas of life and groom a self-disciplined attitude. It will help him or her in this intimate area as well.

For your teen to remain sexually pure it will take a sober-minded, alert-to-danger, conscientious choice. If your teen struggles with addictions, help them create a pattern, a set of actions, they take when they feel temptation coming on. Remind them of *stop, drop, and roll: Stop* whatever you're doing that is causing your desires to be ignited, *drop* to your knees in prayer, and *roll* into the better choice: a walk around the block, a call to an accountability partner, listening to a worship song, exercise, changing rooms in the house to find someone to talk with (about any topic)—any change of scenery or activity will distract them from the compulsion. Help your child set a plan in place before he or she is struggling with temptation and they may avoid the whole negative cycle of indulging sexual urges.

Finally, *keep goals but remove idle time.* When we were in youth work, and while raising our own kids, we saw that a busy teen was a healthy teen. It is just harder for a teen to make a bad choice if his or her days are already scheduled full of good choices. This doesn't mean they have no downtime, but that their time off to relax, rejuvenate, and recover would be more structured or supervised. Overall, we found our sons didn't have time to develop habits to erode their lives because they set, worked for, and reached lofty goals. Work with your child to dream God-sized dreams for his or her life.

First Corinthians 6:12 draws us to the conclusion that we should never settle for being mastered by bad habits: "'I have the right to do anything,' you say—but not everything is beneficial. 'I have the right to do anything'—but I will not be *mastered* by anything." When masturbation or any other habit begins to master or dominate a life, or if your teen plans their schedule around the opportunity to engage in an addictive experience, it is time to get professional counseling.

My Mistakes

To help deter errors like premarital sex, expose your tween or teen to the sobering reality of a life after some of the possible mistakes:

DISEASE	HEALTH CONSEQUENCE
Chlamydia	Produces scar tissue in a woman's sex organs and can leave a woman infertile. One in ten teen girls are currently infected, with 1.5 million cases being added each year.
Gonorrhea	Can scar sex organs and lead to infertility. Leads to arthritis and heart infections. 650,000 new cases each year.
Syphilis	Produces rashes and sores on genitalia. Attacks nervous system and affects eyes, blood, liver, bones, and joints. Can lead to paralysis, blindness, and dementia. Often leads to miscarriage or is passed along to baby.
Genital Herpes	Produces sores on genitalia. A quarter of all Americans have this disease. Very contagious: one in five children over the age of twelve are infected.
Human Papillomavirus (HPV)	Causes infertility, cervical cancer, and premature labor in women. Linked to penile, anal, and other cancers in men. 9.2 million people are currently infected.
Hepatitis B	Produces flu-like symptoms, attacking the liver and kidneys. About 5,000 people die each year due to complications from this chronic infection.
HIV/AIDS	The deadliest known STI, AIDS has killed more Americans than died in WWII. Destroys immune system and renders body incapable of fighting off disease.

All teens seem to think, "It can't happen to me!" So use stories to drive the point home. One young mother came up to me after I spoke at a MOPS meeting. She was sobbing so hard it took a while to help her gain enough composure for her story to tumble out. "It was just one time; just one night. Now everything is tainted," she said. "Each pregnancy I worry about the safety of my baby. Every sexual interaction I worry about my husband. It is a wall between us. He tries to be understanding, but just taking precautions to protect him from my disease is a wall—it stands between us. I hate it! If I had just paid attention to all the good advice, all the warnings, all the adults in my life saying, 'Don't, don't!' I am only twenty-five years old and all I can see for my future is years and years of regret ahead. One day I will have to confront this. I will have to tell my own children. I didn't even love the guy. I didn't even know him, really. And I know he didn't love or care for me. But he gave me a gift that keeps on giving—pain, shame, hopelessness. Such pain. Such shame. Such a waste! I don't even know why I am sharing this. It isn't like you can heal it. I guess I just needed to tell someone. I feel so all alone."

Unplanned Pregnancy

Now, all children are a blessing. Psalm 127:3-5 tells us, "Children are a heritage from the LORD, offspring a reward from him. Like arrows in the hands of a warrior are children born in one's youth. Blessed is the man whose quiver is full of them." Children are a blessing, even unplanned ones—but the timing can make life difficult! With three out of every ten American girls becoming pregnant by the age of 20,[3] you need to use every possible teaching moment to educate your teen about the cost, the work, and the responsibility of parenting a child. Encourage them to work in children's ministry, mission trips for children's causes, youth camps, or Vacation Bible School. Volunteer to have your family care for special needs kids or a single or teen mother. Even making your children be fiscally responsible can clue him or her into the escalating cost of parenthood. Draw up a budget and make your teen responsible for earning and paying for some of their own needs: shoes, clothes, social life, etc. Give them the responsibility of helping clip coupons or helping grocery shop.

If friends, family, or even a television show bring up the topic of teen parenthood, discuss the lifestyle changes that come with the responsibility of having children. Then take steps to move your teen out of the highest risk groups: Teen girls who live with non-parent relatives begin having intercourse at a younger age than those who have always lived with at least one biological parent. One study found that almost one third of girls in foster care become pregnant at least once by age 17. Teenage girls whose boyfriends are in a gang are twice as likely to become pregnant as their peers.[4] Teens in single-parent homes are more likely to become sexually active, as are teens whose parents were unmarried when they themselves were born.[5] The likelihood that teenage girls will become pregnant increases by 11 percent with each change in family structure (parental marriage, divorce, remarriage, etc.). Are you seeing a pattern? Teens most at risk are those without two parents (or an attentive single parent) and in a social setting where teen pregnancy is seen as acceptable or the norm.

There are some choices you can make as a parent that will help your child not to become a statistic. According to the Heritage Foundation, your teen will be less likely to engage in premarital sex if you:

- stay married or keep your marital status stable in his or her teen years
- talk to them about sex
- monitor their activities and behavior
- show them that you disapprove of premarital sex
- allow them to watch less TV than their peers
- talk with them about sex and sexual standards[6]

Answers to Have Ready

Make some notes for a conversation with your tween or teen in each area we have discussed:

Media: Have your child download and complete the Teen Media Contract (available at www.Love-Wise.com).

Friends: Set up a date to discuss expanding or improving your student's peer circle and involvement with teens seeking to live wisely.

Urges: Set up a time to discuss masturbation with your child (this might be more comfortable if Mom talks to daughters and Dad talks to sons).

Mistakes: Set up a time to discuss potential mistakes or missteps to avoid. If you have any adjustments to make in your parenting to help your teen make wiser choices, this is the time to explain what family traditions will be instituted and why.

Parent to Parent

Why should we stand for pro-life? This can be a divisive topic because so many have been touched personally by the decision to choose life…or not. We think this is a pivotal core belief. This is one reason why even the founders of the United States wrote in the Declaration of Independence, "We hold these truths to be self-evident, that all men are created equal, that they are endowed by their Creator with certain unalienable Rights, that among these are Life, Liberty and the pursuit of Happiness."

But there is another document that also raises life as a core value to be cherished. In Psalm 139:13-16 we read,

> For you created my inmost being; you knit me together in my mother's womb. I praise you because I am fearfully and wonderfully made; your works are wonderful, I know that full well. My frame was not hidden from you when I was made in the secret place, when I was woven together in the depths of the earth. Your eyes saw my unformed body; all the days ordained for me were written in your book before one of them came to be.

A person who honors and protects life, the life of the yet unborn, the most innocent of them all, is more likely to honor and protect their own life and the lives of those around them.

The big question science and theology has wrestled with is, "When does life begin?" We taught our children that life begins at the first moment an egg and a sperm unite. From that moment on, all it takes is time and care for a child to be born. That is why we encouraged you to use a beautiful book that included photographs of a baby in the womb when teaching very young children where a baby comes from—and to bring it back out as your kids turn the corner into their teen years. Life is beautiful and those who cherish life have the ability to create beautiful lives and help others do the same.

God sets life in motion. By the eighteenth day of pregnancy the child's heart is already beating. Just a few days later its blood is being pumped through its own separate circulatory system, and the eyes, ears, and respiratory system are developing. Before the two-month mark brain waves can be recorded, the skeleton is complete, and reflexes are present. Their hands, eyelids, toes, and nose develop. The baby begins to kick and can suck its thumb. Every organ is in place, bones begin to replace cartilage, fingerprints begin to form, and the baby can begin to hear.

By the end of the first trimester of pregnancy, the baby can squint, swallow, move his or her tongue, make a fist, frown, and hiccup. Teeth form and tiny fingernails develop. The baby can "breathe" amniotic fluid and urinate. All organ systems are functioning and the baby has all of the parts necessary to experience pain, including nerves, a spinal cord, and a thalamus. Vocal cords are complete. And just a few weeks later, the genitals will form and a parent will know whether the baby is a boy or a girl.

That's life by any standard. Yet one out of three women in the U.S. have an abortion by the time they are forty-five.[7] The reasons most frequently cited for having an abortion were that having a child would interfere with a woman's education, work, or ability to care for dependents; that she could not afford a baby now; and that she did not want to be a single mother or was having relationship problems.[8] None of these reasons would be grounds for a mother to kill her already born child, yet we reach inside the womb and justify the action before birth. In addition, the choice for abortion in cases of rape and incest are less than one percent.[9] And in the only major study of pregnant rape victims ever done prior to this book, Dr. Sandra Mahkorn found that 75 to 85 percent did not have abortions.[10] To the victim, an abortion seemed just another form of violence against them.

Abortion to save the life of the mother is a rare case, a dilemma nearly made obsolete due to the great advancements in medicine. Jasper Williams, Jr., a past president of the National Medical Association, says that, "Doctors now have the tools and the knowledge with which to work so that they can handle almost any disease a patient might have…without interrupting the pregnancy."[11] Physicians on both sides of the debate concur on this but the strongest evidence may be from a pro-choice physician who said, "The idea of abortion to save the mother's life is something that people cling to because it sounds noble and pure—but medically speaking, it probably doesn't exist. It's a real stretch of our thinking."[12]

The Association of Prolife Physicians explains, "When the life of the mother is truly threatened by her pregnancy, if both lives cannot simultaneously be saved, then saving the mother's life must be the primary aim. If through our careful treatment of the mother's illness the preborn patient inadvertently dies or is injured, this is tragic and, if unintentional, is not unethical and is consistent with the pro-life ethic."[13]

So in the vast majority of cases, a child's *inconvenience* to the life of the mother is the main reason women elect to abort. We have to help women think through their choices because they sometimes lose the ability to process rationally. For example, in one study of those who had an abortion, more than a third of interview respondents said they had considered adoption and concluded that it was a morally unconscionable option because giving one's child away is wrong.[14] This is an outrageous conclusion. Simply put it means these women think it is morally right to kill a baby, but it is morally wrong to allow that same baby to live and allow a loving family to raise it.

In nine out of ten cases economics is the driving fear, and women can't picture how to provide for themselves while pregnant or for a baby after birth.[15] When we support these girls, alleviate their fears with tangible help, and give them alternatives like adoption, it does help women make better choices.

One mistake—one wrong choice to have premarital sex that results in a pregnancy—is not a reason to compound the problem with more poor choices. Pushing a young couple to marry too young (without adequate premarital counseling) will make matters worse and is not worth saving face socially. Pressuring marriage before helping them mature to economically support themselves will not fix the problem but compound it. In addition, pushing abortion destroys a person—the baby—but it can also emotionally destroy a mother with long-range consequences like depression, infertility, sexual dysfunction, and other more subtle side effects. To value life, even an unplanned life, will be the road out of chaos and back to stability. If the choice is made to care for the mother and the baby, the best option will rise to the surface because this is the stand nearer to the heart of God.

We openly discussed abortion and life with our children, and our sons participated in pro-life events with us so they could become equipped to help their peers if they should find themselves in a hard situation. We tangibly supported mothers with baby showers, childcare, and other practical help. We also looked for heroic examples of love to hold up to our children, examples of courage, like these two women, conceived of a rape:

> Rebecca Wasser-Kiessling, who was conceived in a rape, is rightfully proud of her mother's courage and generosity and wisely reminds us of a fundamental truth that transcends biological paternity: "I believe that God rewarded my birth mother for the suffering she endured, and that I am a gift to her. The serial rapist is not my creator; God is."
>
> Similarly, Julie Makimaa, who works diligently against the perception that abortion is acceptable or even necessary in cases of sexual assault, proclaims, "It doesn't matter how I began. What matters is who I will become."[16]

When you raise your tweens and teens to honor and value life, it carries over to other areas. Your sons will be the protectors of the girls and women of their world. The women in all of our sons' lives have shared how they have gone out of their way to ensure that all the women of their social circle arrive home safely, even if it meant them walking them to their car, walking them across campus to their dorm, or rescuing them if a tire went flat. Your son could become a protector of women—a doctor, lawyer, politician, pastor, or just a really great husband someday—because you chose to help him value life. All life.

In addition, many of the girls I have mentored are in the trenches of the pro-life movement every day, simply voicing reason and giving their friends good wisdom like, "Don't have sex. Choose life. Don't drink. Let me call your mom. Let me take you home. You have value. Don't let him talk to you that way. Let me get you someplace safe…" Your daughter could become a doctor, lawyer, midwife, youth worker, mentor, politician, or a really great friend, and one day, after marriage, a really great mother herself, because you helped her embrace the value of life. If we equip our teens, they will be the watchmen not only over their own lives, but over the lives of their generation.

Answers for Your Heart

If a third of women have an abortion, many moms reading this book might be among that number. If you are one of them, do not carry this pain, this burden, this secret alone any longer. Pat Layton has written a wonderful resource for women, *Surrendering the Secret*, that can set you and your family free. Often your local crisis pregnancy clinic or your local church offers these types of abortion recovery programs.

Some of my best friends have turned their own pain into an outreach to rescue and redeem others. Musician Gwen Smith's story, *Broken into Beautiful*, may also be a source of comfort. Tammy DeAmas, the director of alternatives women's center, traded her shame, guilt, and pain in for God's mercy and grace. This past year over 250 babies were saved because her staff gave the kind of accurate information she was not given. In addition, her own teens and college-aged children are making wise choices for their own future because she and her husband were brave enough to deal with their past. Mom and Dad, turn your past into a path of hope for your own children and the teens of your community. The truth will set you free.

Can You Guide Me to My Future?

Therefore, my brothers and sisters, you whom I love and long for, my joy and crown, stand firm in the Lord in this way, dear friends!

Philippians 4:1

Mom and Dad, your job is to gently, strategically, thoughtfully, and purposefully release—one finger at a time—the grip you hold on your son or daughter's life. Roll the relationship ball into his or her court. Work yourself out of a job and prepare him or her to invite someone into their life as a marriage partner. As parents, we need to equip our kids to have an epic love story that will pass down from generation to generation as a heritage from the Lord.

To accomplish this mission, you need to put on your glasses of faith. Many of us have or will soon need to get reading glasses or bifocals, and the optometrist will ask us during the exam, "Is this clearer? Or this?" Life and love are always going to be clearer when you look through the lenses of faith.

So take a moment and write down in your journal a description of your son or daughter on his or her wedding day. If you form a partnership with God, working to apply all the principles discussed in this book, that precious day will happen with God's best partner in God's best timing. Hang on to this picture of hope by faith, in the days between now and that wedding day. It will not help to dwell on a son or daughter's failures, fumblings, and false starts. Look at your child through the lenses of faith, and God will give you light for the next step on your path. He will give wisdom to your child too as he or she stays tied to the heart of God.

The Flashlight

We were at the beach with a group, singing by the campfire, and when we left to head back to our room we discovered we were not adequately prepared. It was pitch-black and no moon was out that night. We could not see the path through the chest-high grass between our spot on the beach and the beach cottage destination. Then one of the men, seeing our dilemma, said, "I just got a smartphone and I have a flashlight app. I will lead you." With the light, the trip back seemed simple and easy.

In the same way, when we were youth pastors we saw many families struggling, arguing, and wasting precious family time in episodes of drama with their children. They too needed an app to light up the path to relationship wellness. They needed God's light to sort through relationship issues as a united team rather than combating them as enemies. We sat down and drafted the Teen Relationship Contract and began holding yearly relationship and parenting seminars. Our goal was to help families unite and work together in more positive ways.

Many of our tools from these seminars are available at our website. They help you and your teen answer questions like…

- What does God say about relationships?
- Who should I marry (and date)?
- When am I responsible enough to date?
- How shall I date? Where should I go (or not) and what should I do (or not)?
- What role do parents play in all this?
- How can I avoid toxic relationships or unhealthy people?
- How far should I go physically?

- As things get more serious, how do I move the relationship forward in a healthy way?

- How do I know and how do I rightly handle a relationship that needs to end because we are not right as future marriage partners?

- Who will pay for dates? And transport me to a date?

- How can I avoid temptation, dangerous situations, or foolish decisions in relationships?

- When is it time for solo dating rather than double or group dates and activities?

- How do you meet quality people? How do you know who is a quality person and how can I be a quality person who handles relationships well?

- What do I do when I believe I have found "the one"?

The most important question the parent of a teen should learn to ask is, "Tell me, why should I say yes?" Then roll the ball into their court and have them present a case for their decision. So when they ask, "Can I date?" don't answer yes or no. Instead, ask, "Tell me, why should I say yes?" and hand them the Teen Relationship Contract. Let them wrestle with the myriad of issues to land at a place where they own their convictions about how God wants them to handle relationships.

Defining Relationships from God's Point of View

The terms *dating* and *courtship* are man-made words aimed at helping people get a handle on the wide variety of relationship choices and decisions. In addition, parents should keep themselves aware of what trendy terms are emerging and what teens or young adults might mean when they say they are "going together," "going out," "hooking up," or "friends with benefits." Some of these are just euphemisms for connecting romantically, while others are direct references to sex with no commitments or responsibilities. If you hear or see any term you don't understand or are unsure of, do your research! In this final section, we are going to attempt to remove all of man's terminology and simply look at how God runs relationships. These will be the foundational principles that you can use to equip your son or daughter to follow God's path to marriage.

Individual Responsibility and Maturity

We often get the question, "At what age is it okay to allow our son or daughter to date?" We usually respond with a question of our own: "What do you see as the purpose of dating?" Some people see dating as entertainment, like golf or tennis. We happen to believe that dating is a process of finding out if this is the right person to marry. If that is the case, one would only need to begin solo dating (not in a group) if he or she is ready to begin the process of selecting a marriage partner (a process some call courtship).

This often then leads to the question, "Is there a better age to marry?" and studies say that there is. Here are a few bits of information to log away for a time when your child is ready to decide on marriage.

Marriage Prime Time

Recent research by sociologist Norval Glenn found that couples who married between 23 and 27 reported greater satisfaction with their marriages than those who married before and after them, and that those marriages are less likely to break up than those who marry in the later twenties (or marry before age 20).[1] Focus on the Family concurs that the prime age is 22 to 25. An "earlier" marriage in the early twenties increases the likelihood of couples marrying as virgins, which is an important factor in marital stability and happiness. The 22 to 25 range of age at first marriage seems to be that which enhances both the quality and stability of marriage.[2]

The current age for the first marriage is higher than it has been since World War II, but not for a good reason: In a 1946 Gallup poll, most found the ideal age to be 25 for men and 21 for women. Sixty years later, in a Gallup poll the ideal age had increased to 25 for women and 27 for men.[3] Premarital cohabitation contributed to the delay. From 1960 to 2011, the number of cohabitating couples jumped from 430,000 to 7.6 million.[4]

The biological clock is also a consideration. As Sharon Jayson puts it, "Fertility researcher Richard Paulson of the University of Southern California says that, as a general rule, women should start having children no later than age 30 and be done by 35, when statistics show fertility declines."[5]

Some of our friends, professors at a seminary, were married at nineteen. They told our 21-year-old son and his 20-year-old bride, "It isn't how old you are; it's how committed you are." And we agree. We know couples in midlife who are less mature than our son and his wife were on their wedding day. And we know couples of all ages and all income brackets who wouldn't know what commitment is if it walked in the door and shook their hand.

But there are some basic commonsense parameters. Do you have enough education to support yourself and your spouse? If you marry now, can you better achieve both of your goals and God's call on your life? Will marrying help you maintain your integrity? When we hear of couples delaying wedding dates because they can't afford a wedding, we know priorities are askew. An actual wedding is very inexpensive: a license, a pastor, and a place to wed (which can be a home or home church). It is the *party* that is expensive. If more time and energy is going into the wedding and the reception than is going into the premarital training and the relationship, no matter how old the couple is, this is not a healthy sign of commitment. Much of the world's culture values a lavish party over purity. Relationship expert and pastor Mark Gungor says, "If young adult couples say they want to get married, parents should support them, even if they're still in college. How can we tell young people that living together and premarital sex lowers their chances for a happy marriage, and then say wait to marry until 28? What do you think you've just set up?"[6]

One of the best places to meet a future spouse is college, especially a Christian college, or on one of the opportunities offered during college like mission trips and Christian clubs. Most people graduate college around age 22. Given a year to establish some kind of income if that wasn't accomplished in college and get the premarital training, mentoring, and basic wedding plans accomplished, age 23 is not out of the question. (Having a college degree does lower the rate of divorce.) If a young person is able to provide, choose a mate wisely, and live out his or her call, a marriage could happen earlier in life (as is the case with many in the military). We told our kids that their age wasn't as important as their readiness to provide, their desire to remain pure before marriage, and their ability to wisely select a mate. Our financial help for college was not tied to their marital status; it was tied to their choice to maintain integrity.

The Dating Window

So with mid-twenties established as the overall best time for marriage, we can begin to address the original question: When should you start dating? How long does it take to really get to know if someone is right for you? We encourage couples to spend at least a year together. This will allow them to meet each other's friends and family and see how they function under stress and how they manage life when the pressure is off. It is also healthy for a couple to go on several dates that include ministry and service so one can see how well they can serve God as a couple. With most people this process takes at least a year and often two or even three, especially if they do not live in the same city. This pushes the dating window back to the ages of 17 to 21.

In our home, we thought a son was not ready to date until several factors were in place. First, he had to show responsibility in the major areas of life—grades, chores, and keeping their promises. Second, he had to have his own source of income (since we weren't going to fund dates). Third, since we weren't chauffeurs, he had to have a car to drive, gas in that car, and a license to drive with another person in the car. It is a proof of maturity to arrange your own driver's education, and in some families this might include paying for the classes, the car, the insurance, the fees, etc. (In metro areas, you can require your son to navigate mass transit or pay for a date's taxi ride.) Finally, the son needed to meet with the young woman's family, explain his Relationship Contract, and explain how he planned on keeping their daughter pure.

The soonest these things could all be accomplished was around age 17. This was the age that they could begin to pursue a special or exclusive relationship (and show through handling group dates then double dates well that they could then go to the parents of the girl and ask to solo date her). Even after they gained permission to date alone, we still encouraged the majority of interactions in a relationship be in groups or with family members. That's a more realistic portrayal of what life is: a series of interactions in the larger context of family, friendships, a church, and a community.

Before all these things were accomplished, our teens were welcome to invite friends of the opposite sex to any church activity or Christian group and they were welcome to accept invitations from a girl's family. Groups are good!

Studies back up a more conservative dating age. Dr. Jim Burns shows that 91 percent of children who begin dating at age 12 will no longer be virgins at their high school graduation. If they delay dating until at least age 16, the percentage drops to 20.[7]

Give God Maximum Glory and Have Maximum Influence on the Kingdom

We tell our audiences exactly what we told our own kids: "Your partner is on the path to your passion." This means we equip our children to pursue God wholeheartedly rather than chasing relationships. When a young person passionately pursues God's path, they will meet and make connections with someone who is on the same journey. As each pursues the plan He has placed on their hearts, God will intersect their paths. God is a master chessman, the best of matchmakers, and He connects people so that His will for the world is accomplished.

When your son or daughter pursues that special someone, it should be because he or she can see how together they can be better servants for God. God's intent is to build couples and families that are strong, healthy, and vibrant so they can be a landing spot, a safe place, an oasis of hope, a training ground for their future children but also for those around them at work, in their community, and in society.

Protect the Heart and Future of All Involved

We have questions in the Teen Relationship Contract that help a teen think through things like gifts, active over passive dating, and more vital concerns like how relationships gain intimacy and the amount of time spent talking heart to heart. But most vital is how physical touch is managed. Sexual promiscuity is not a harmless, victimless activity.

What you will see missing from this chapter is a list of contraception options. The world thinks safe sex means pregnancy prevention methods, or maybe some options to prevent STIs. However, no contraception will protect the emotions, the heart, and the mind. In addition, contraception is not the "safe" path as the world preaches it to be. Condoms often fail and cannot be relied upon to protect against pregnancy and disease. Condom use means you are playing Russian Roulette with your life. "Safe sex" is not all that safe. The only way to make it safe is to save it for marriage.

Hooking Up or Hooked?

Why is sexual integrity so hard to find in this society? People are hooked on sex. Here is the science of it: This fascinating process is clearly visible with modern brain scan technology, revealing different areas of the brain lighting up. Sexual activity releases dopamine, a "feel good" chemical. Dopamine rewards us by flooding our brains and making the brain cells produce a feeling of excitement or of well-being. It makes us feel the need to repeat pleasurable, exciting, and rewarding acts.

It should be noted, however, that dopamine is values-neutral. In other words, it is an involuntary response that cannot tell right from wrong. The doctors continue to explain that sex is one of the strongest generators of dopamine, so people are vulnerable to falling into a cycle of dopamine reward for unwise sexual behavior—they can get hooked on it.

This feeling is created by God to enhance marital stability, but for singles it can cause a person to attach to someone who might not be healthy for them. If a person decides that he does not want to attach to the same partner over and over, but is addicted to the rush of sex that dopamine creates, he might go from partner to partner. When this action is repeated it can cause his or her brain to mold and gel so that it eventually begins to accept this sexual pattern as normal, damaging their ability to bond in a committed relationship.

The Cohabitation Lie

Sex outside of marriage leads to an attitude of compromise. You might have heard someone say, "Marriage is just a piece of paper." This might be a good line of reasoning except for a few compelling facts:

- Sex can bond you to an unhealthy person. If you have had many sexual partners prior to living with this one, then your brain is still patterned to love and leave.

- The majority of cohabitating couples describe their relationship as "on the rocks."

- Cohabitating couples are twice as likely to divorce compared to those who did not live together prior to marriage.

- Cohabitating couples are more prone to violence.

- Cohabitating couples are four times more likely to cheat than those who marry.

- Cohabitating couples tend to move in together before knowing each other well, so there can be errors in judgment on selecting a partner.

- Cohabitating couples are more likely to produce children and this can place undue stress on a relationship that has yet to be rooted and strengthened.

- The effect of cohabitation on children is vast. Children in cohabiting homes are 20 times more likely to be abused and are 22 times more likely to be incarcerated as an adult than a child from an intact home. [8]

- Cohabiting couples have love that is temporary: Only one in six will stay together three years, and only one in ten will last ten years or more. Most cohabiting couples, in fact, will last a mere 18 months. [9]

It has been our experience as pastors and as relationship specialists that the majority of people who cohabitate do not end up getting married. A few do, and a few of those stay married, but they are defying the odds. There are a few reasons why living together is counterproductive to long-term love. First, you are deciding together to disobey God. This is not a great start or a strong foundation to build on. Second, you are deciding to *not* decide on the key issue that will move your future forward. Are you willing to place all your eggs in this relationship basket, knowing that your partner could move to another city, move to another partner, move to another residence at a moment's notice and there will be little recourse available to you? Finally, you are not really trying out the relationship because it is not the same as marriage. Living with a back door open, an escape hatch, an exit plan, is not the same as marriage. If testing the relationship is the goal, cohabitation will not help you discern it in a realistic way.

Purity in All Areas of Life

Sexual integrity isn't formed in a vacuum; it is the natural outgrowth of a pure heart and a life of integrity in all areas. One of the most important parts of the Teen Relationship Contract is the *How Far Should I Go?* chart, explaining God's view of the most-asked question we get from teenagers: "How far can I go?"

It is actually the wrong question. It shouldn't be *How far can I go and then be outside of God's will*? It should instead be *How close can I get to the heart of God and how would that be reflected in my relationships?* God doesn't play with people's hearts and emotions. When God reaches out in love, it is a clearly defined relationship: "For God so loved the world that he gave his one and only Son, that whoever believes in him shall not perish but have eternal life" (John 3:16).

Ask your son or daughter to answer this before God: "How far back do you need to push your line to maintain a pure heart toward the person you are in relationship with and a pure heart toward God?" We know that sex actually begins where foreplay begins (and oral sex is sex), so the line should push back to petting outside of clothes at a minimum. However, the switch is ignited for most people at "making out." It is easy to get lost in the passionate kisses, lost in the moment. The flesh, the lust, the craving can easily take over making it difficult to pull back.

How far am I willing to go?

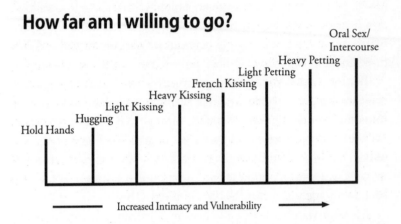

Increased Intimacy and Vulnerability

Let us share a personal example from our own love story. When we first started dating, I (Pam) came to a crossroads in my relationship with God. I had made a list of the kind of person I wanted to someday marry by listing traits I saw in the New Testament in Christ and His disciples. It was a list of internal character qualities: loving, respectful of women, a good listener, kind and compassionate. Bill fit the list. Our hearts and plans were running in the same direction, but because we were allowing God to rework our dating patterns we were both in new territory emotionally. One week in my quiet time, I became impressed with the fact that on the following weekend when I saw Bill, I would need to know where I stood on areas of physical boundaries. I knew my past pattern of letting the guy take the lead wasn't very wise, so I let God take the lead this time. I studied and saw the verses that backed up my decision to remain a virgin. But I also saw a pattern, and as I prayed I became convinced that our physical relationship needed to progress forward only after tangible measures of commitment. When God said, "I love you," He demonstrated it! I thought that was a good principle! That weekend Bill and I sat on a rock in the sunshine and talked for hours as we watched the ocean. It was one of the best days of my life. I felt so cherished, so loved, so wanted. Bill had a list of questions he wanted to ask me about and they mostly concerned our physical boundaries. How far did we think God wanted us to go and when? We navigated our conversation through, holding hands, hugging, walking arm in arm. We'd already decided God was clear about no sex before marriage—it was all the stuff in between we were concerned and confused about now. I knew God had prepared me for that weekend.

Bill took me to my friends' apartment where I was staying to get ready for our evening date. And that evening was magical too—a quiet, romantic fondue dinner and a walk through the downtown district over bridges and creeks and under gas lamps on a foggy night. We walked and talked and talked and walked. I was getting cold so Bill wrapped his arms around me and tucked me into his car to take me back to my friends'. Before he did, he asked, "Pam, can I kiss you?"

My body wanted to rush into his arms and let him kiss me over and over again, but the Holy Spirit inside me reminded me of my quiet time conversations with God that I had journalled all week.

"Bill, I want to say yes, but I can't. You are so godly, so incredibly gorgeous, and I really want to say yes! But I've wrecked all my past relationships because I haven't watched over this area of my life very well. I'm afraid if I start kissing you I won't be able to stop there. I value my relationship with you too much to kiss you. So until you're ready to commit to me as the person you'd like to marry, then I have to say no. I care for you a lot but I care for God more…so…."

I trailed off as he stared at me in silence. He brushed my tear-stained cheek with fingertips for a brief moment, took my hand and drove me home in utter silence for 20 minutes.

I told him again at the door what a wonderful day I had had with him and how much I loved being with him, and he mumbled something about picking me up for breakfast. I opened the door and burst into tears. My girlfriends rushed toward me. "What's wrong? What's wrong?"

I blurted out, "I am so afraid I might have said goodbye to the best man I've ever had in my life!" I explained the story of how I knew God had been preparing me and I had a choice, Bill's will or God's will, and I chose God.

One of my friends tried to comfort me. "Pam, we all know Bill and that he wants God's best in his life and in yours. You have to trust his character. If he really is the godly man he appears to be, he'll handle this."

Another said, "God led you to this decision so He has to have a reason—trust the heart of God!"

The group of us prayed together. They slept and I lay awake a while longer, wondering what morning's light would bring.

Bill was smiling when he picked me up in the morning. "Pam, I didn't say anything last night because I didn't know what to say. I've never been in the presence of a woman as committed to God as you are. Just being with you strengthens my walk with God. Pam, I was hurt and embarrassed last night. I felt like I should have been the one who protected our purity—that's why I was quiet. But I want you to know I totally agree with you. You are the best thing that has ever happened to me and I don't want our relationship to crumble because we didn't watch over our sexuality. I won't play games with your heart. When I am ready to marry you, then I will ask to kiss you."

A few months later, at the same beach house where Bill first asked me for a kiss, he bent on his knee, sang a song he wrote especially for me, and asked me to marry him. I of course said, "Yes!" Then he asked, "May I kiss you?"

"Yes!" I cried. And it was a kiss worth waiting for.

The Best Payoff for a Parent

The best part of choosing God's path is that years later the fruit continues to grow. Let's use our oldest son, Brock, as an example. He signed the relationship contract and each year we would meet and he'd update us on his plan to stay true to the standards God had called him to. His love story has become an epic tale of romance.

We had sent Brock's profile to a host of highly competitive schools. Being an undersized quarterback meant he needed a miracle to get a scholarship despite his record-breaking performances. In answer to his prayers, Liberty University called. We all celebrated as he signed his letter of intent. Since Brock's birth, we have prayed for his future bride. When Brock had been at Liberty just a few days, I spoke at a book signing event at a bookstore in Phoenix, Arizona. I struck up a conversation with the owner and his wife, Sheryl. She asked me, "Where did you say Brock got his scholarship?"

"He's the quarterback at Liberty University," I replied.

"Our Hannah goes to Liberty!" she said.

We gave the kids each other's phone numbers and our two strong-willed, firstborn kids decided to go on a date! After eighteen months of dating and a week in fasting and prayer, Brock took Hannah on a "tour" of their relationship, a visit to meaningful places. To safeguard their purity, they had not even kissed yet.

At the place they first met Brock gave Hannah nails. At the place they first talked seriously, he gave her a hammer. At the place they first prayed, he gave her a piece of wood. Finally, at the home she was living in with friends, he gave her a second piece of wood, which they hammered together to form a cross. He knelt on one knee next to the cross and said, "I want our relationship to start at the foot of the cross. Hannah, will you marry me?"

Brock and Hannah tied the knot and became husband and wife. Brock is now a football coach and educator, building into teens those same leadership qualities we prayed over and poured into him. Hannah is the amazing mother of our grandchildren and a leader serving in women's ministry. Together they are changing the world around them for Christ.

Our second son married his beautiful bride with a heart for God while we were writing this book. We asked our two daughters-in-law to comment on how we raised our sons—if they thought it produced the kind of man they are glad they married. Here are their answers:

> **Hannah:** I don't think I can put the payoffs into one quote. It would take a novel to summarize the benefits of being married to a Farrel. For our anniversary, I came up with 84 things that I respected about Brock. One for each month

we've been married. What's crazy is that it was *easy* to come up with that many things. I bet most wives aren't blessed like the Farrel wives are.

Caleigh: Marrying a man who values his relationships as his top priority is the biggest blessing I could ever ask for! Zach tells me almost every day that he wants to make an impact on anyone that comes in his life. He follows this by saying, "As a couple, I want us to make that same impact on every couple we come in contact with! It is our goal to show people our love for one another and our passion to have such a STRONG relationship!"

If we teach our kids to give God glory in their lives and relationships, God will write a beautiful love story.

Answers to Have Ready

Parents can be divided into two categories—those who need to step up and those who need to step back.

Step Up

If you use the Teen Relationship Contract and Media Contract and mix in an ample sampling of celebrations, your relationship with your child will become strong and satisfying as you watch him or her make wise choices. Some parents think all the contracts, all the planned discussions, all the oversight of commitments, and all the time, money, and effort for so many celebrations is just too much work. It is work—lots of work.

But neglecting these responsibilities can actually turn into more work, more effort, and more expense. Being your kid's relationship warden is not much fun and extremely stressful. To wait up late at night wondering and worrying about where your teen is—that's work. Calling all your teen's friends because your kid didn't come home last night—that's more work. Nailing their window shut so he or she can't sneak out, taking their keys, paying for weeks of counseling to help straighten out the life they have made a mess of—that is definitely work. Raising your grandchild because your teen bailed on his or her responsibilities—that is *mountains* of work. Yes, this book is packed with work—but you'll find fruit for your labor! You have to plant the crop to reap the harvest; you have to tend the vineyard to taste the sweet, abundant fruit. It's worth the work.

Step Back

There are two ways to parent—by fear or by faith. There comes a time when you need to trust your parenting. There is such a thing as hanging on too tight and too long. We have seen some parents so paralyzed with trying to get this area right that they do wrong—fear is not healthy.

The Bible is clear that we are to live by faith. Faith has confidence instead of control. Faith directs instead of dictates. Faith liberates instead of locking down and latching on. We have seen families who have strong, peaceful relationships with their children become contentious, frustrated, and filled with drama much in part to mom and dad refusing to let go. The Bible gives clear reminders to parents. Ephesians 6:4 says, "Fathers, do not exasperate your children; instead, bring them up in the training and instruction of the Lord." And Proverbs 14:1 tells us that "The wise woman builds her house, but with her own hands the foolish one tears hers down."

We have seen parents build not just a hedge around their children but an electric fence, with barbed wire and armed guards. It might keep evil out, but it can also keep sane, emotionally healthy, loving, godly, quality potential mates out too. If your rules are so rigorous, so domineering that healthy people, quality Christians, or church leaders see them as exasperating, you could be hanging on too tight.

We've come across some rules over the years that we concluded were unhealthy, unproductive, and unwarranted. There was the mother who wouldn't allow her college-age son, attending one of the most prestigious universities of the nation, to go on any dates without her. Then there were the parents who wouldn't let their daughter (a college graduate who had a professional career) go on a date without a written agenda, a pre-approved married couple to act as chaperones, and separate transportation arranged. Or the father who pulled a Laban, promising a young man that he would give his daughter in marriage after five years of weekly mentoring meetings. At the end of the fifth year he said he was still not comfortable and told the man at least two more years of weekly prayer meetings would be necessary for the hand of his daughter (who was nearly 30 at this point).

There are three outcomes we have observed when parents hold on too tightly for too long. The first is that the daughter or son acquiesces to the regulations but their spirit is extracted. They lose their ability to make decisions in other areas of their life, becoming stunted in their maturity and fearful about taking full responsibility for their life. The second is they rebel against the overzealous rules, pulling away to find their own path to live and serve Jesus. This often includes distancing themselves from the manipulations, controls, and overbearing parents. In this case, the one thing the parent longs for—a close relationship with his or her kids—becomes an impossibility, and it was all self-induced pain. The worst outcome is that they rebel not just against the rules and rigors, not just against their overbearing parents, but against God, seeing Him as the cause of all their emotional pain and chaos.

We pray that you will have faith that God is in control, love that is strong enough to trust, and hope that believes the best about a wise son or daughter. Trust so you can see the blessing of God on your son or daughter—and over you.

Parent to Parent

One of my joys is to see fruit from our books inspire more fruit. That is what happened when Naomi Shedd read my book *Got Teens?* She highlighted, marked up, applied, and morphed many of the ideas into her own family, in her own way, in her own style. She is a creative mom married to a godly man, Tim, and together they have created a wonderful tradition that almost any family could adapt: Shedd Sunday Shenanigans. Every Sunday afternoon, their family plans a fun yet purposeful adventure. If any of their teen and college-age kids were dating someone, they were invited to the Sunday Shenanigans. Naomi and Tim believe (as do we) that people are their authentic selves when interacting with their family, so more can be discovered about the fit of a potential partner in the laboratory of family life.

Shenanigans can be simple, like cooking or barbeques to all-day adventures like hiking, biking, jet skiing, or ministry service projects. For example, on one shenanigan, the family (with their dates) all went to a pottery studio and each made a clay creation. Her son discovered he was in love with a very patient young lady who wanted to take her time and produce a quality product while he wanted to just get it done and get on with other activities he deemed more fun. These are the kind of tidbits that help people decide to make a relationship work or find someone better suited. One way to put it is, "They are both good people; just not good together." This kind of natural setting helps our kids gain this type of vital information.

Like the Shedds, we found that our sons and the young women they wanted to get to know and pursue a relationship with actually liked spending time with us. We did enjoyable activities and we'd often invite our sons and their dates along—or they would plan outings and invite us. Nothing was forced or required. We just have a strong relationship with our sons and we really enjoy the young women they have invited into their lives, and they enjoy us. Our sons had no reason to rebel and no need to pull away because we gave them plenty of room to own and be responsible for their lives.

Answers for Your Heart

You might be wondering, "How can I tell my child to maintain the boundaries that I violated?" You are not a hypocrite if that's what you are thinking. You are human and imperfect. Welcome to the human race—we all are imperfect. But if your life has been redeemed, you have moved your family from darkness to God's loving light. God took ashes and turned it to beauty. Your relationship with God is its own love story, and God is loving you so you can love your son or daughter.

We each have a love story. Tell your love story truthfully, honestly, and in such a way that God gets the glory. When you tell your story, it prepares your son or daughter to live out God's love story for his or her own life.

If you made mistakes and you wonder when to share the imperfections and lessons learned from doing it hard rather than smart, we suggest you share that part of your story by the time your children are the same age you were when you made the mistake. For example, I (Bill) lived near Hollywood as a junior higher and my friendship circle was a group of boys who wallpapered a "fort" with pornography. There are images, conversations, and moments in that fort I wish had never been put into my brain. So late in my own sons' puberty I made sure they knew what to do if any of their friends tempted them to look at porn. And I (Pam) was the daughter of an alcoholic dad, so as a high schooler, I was desperate for love. I was one of those high-maintenance girls I have prayed *out* of my own sons' lives. Before my boys headed to high school, I shared how to spot a brokenhearted woman and how to help her (but not date her).

We all want our children to have a better life than we have had. By telling your story, you give God an opportunity to build into theirs.

You have read about being a watchman to help guard your child's well-being and train them to make wise choices. To solidify this decision to be a heroic parent, please read and sign this commitment before God:

I commit, as a parent and hero to my children, to walk with God in integrity and teach my children to do the same so that the light of God's love burns brighter in our world.

I know I cannot control all my children's choices, but as much as I can I will seek to inform and pray for them, encouraging them to make wise and discerning decisions.

I choose to partner with God because I love my children.

Signed _____

Date _____

Notes

Chapter One

1. Steven C. Martino et al., "Beyond the 'Big Talk': The Roles of Breadth and Repetition in Parent-Adolescent Communication About Sexual Topics," *Pediatrics* 121, no. 3 (March 1, 2008): 612-18, doi: 10.1542/peds.2007-2156.

2. This story is also related in Pam Farrel and Doreen Hanna's book *Raising a Modern-Day Princess* (Carol Stream, IL: Tyndale, 2009), 15-16.

3. "Sexual Risk Behavior: HIV, STD, & Teen Pregnancy Prevention," Centers for Disease Control and Prevention, last modified July 24, 2012, http://www.cdc.gov/healthyyouth/sexualbe haviors/index.htm.

4. Anugrah Kumar, "How Many Evangelical Young Adults Have Sex Before Marriage? Study: Almost Everyone," *Christianity Today Australia*, September 29, 2011, http://au.christiantoday. com/article/how-many-evangelical-young-adults-have-sex-before-marriage-study-almost-everyone/12113.htm.

5. Jason DeParle and Sabrina Tavernise, "For Women Under 30, Most Births Occur Outside Marriage," *The New York Times*, February 17, 2012, http://www.nytimes.com/2012/02/18/us /for-women-under-30-most-births-occur-outside-marriage.html.

6. "Abortion Facts," The Center for Bio-Ethical Reform, accessed September 25, 2012, http:// abortionno.org/Resources/fastfacts.html.

7. "National Reproductive Health Profile," Guttmacher Institute, accessed September 25, 2012, http://www.guttmacher.org/datacenter/profiles/US.jsp.

8. "Facts About Sexual Assault," New York City Alliance Against Sexual Assault, accessed September 25, 2012, http://listen.nycagainstrape.org/learn.html.

9. "Sexually Transmitted Diseases," Epigee Women's Health, accessed September 25, 2012, http:// www.epigee.org/guide/stds.html.

10. "HIV Among Youth," Centers for Disease Control and Prevention, last modified December 2, 2011, http://www.cdc.gov/hiv/youth/index.htm.

11. Daniel Villarreal, "Can We Please Just Start Admitting That We *Do* Actually Want to Indoctrinate Kids?", Queerty, May 12, 2011, http://www.queerty.com/can-we-please-just-start-admitting-that-we-do-actually-want-to-indoctrinate-kids-20110512/.

12. Rebecca Hagelin, "Parents, Teens and Sex," Crosswalk, October 7, 2009, http://www
    .crosswalk.com/family/parenting/parents-and-sex-11610386.html.

13. Miriam Grossman, *You're Teaching My Child What? A Physician Exposes the Lies of Sex Educa-
    tion and How They Harm Your Child* (Washington, DC: Regnery Publishing, Inc., 2009), 1-2.

14. Ibid., 3.

15. Committee on Public Education, "Sexuality, Contraception, and the Media," *Pediatrics* 107,
    no. 1 (January 2001): 191-94, doi: 10.1542/peds.107.1.191.

16. Dave Currie, "Indecent Exposure: Winning the Sexual Battle for the Minds and Hearts of the
    Next Generation," *Doing Family Right,* April 18, 2012, http://www.doingfamilyright.com
    /indecent-exposure-winning-the-sexual-battle-for-the-minds-and-hearts-of-the-next
    -generation/.

17. Ibid.

18. Grossman, *You're Teaching My Child What?*, 7-8.

19. Amy Kramer, "Girl Talk: What High School Senior Girls Have to Say About Sex, Love, and
    Relationships," The National Campaign to Prevent Teen and Unplanned Pregnancy, accessed
    September 26, 2012, www.thenationalcampaign.org/resources/pdf/pubs/girl-talk.pdf, 15.

20. "Parents' Influence on Adolescents' Sexual Behavior," The Heritage Foundation, accessed Sep-
    tember 26, 2012, http://www.familyfacts.org/briefs/42 parents-influence-on-adolescents
    -sexual-behavior.

21. "Teen Sexual Behavior," The Heritage Foundation, accessed September 26, 2012, http://www
    .familyfacts.org/briefs/12/teen-sexual-behavior.

22. Grossman, *You're Teaching My Child What?*, 6.

23. "That's What He Said: What Guys Think About Sex, Love, Contraception, and Relationships,"
    The National Campaign to Prevent Teen and Unplanned Pregnancy, accessed September 26,
    2012, http://www.thenationalcampaign.org/resources/pdf/pubs/ThatsWhatHeSaid.pdf, 14.

24. Stan and Brenna Jones, *How and When to Tell Your Kids About Sex* (Colorado Springs, CO:
    NavPress, 2007), 157.

25. Melina Bersamin et al., "Parenting Practices and Adolescent Sexual Behavior: A Longi-
    tudinal Study," *Journal of Marriage and Family* 70, no. 1 (February 2008): 97-112, doi:
    10.1111/j.1741-3737.2007.00464.x.

Chapter Two

1. Ken Johnson, speaking at the Fellowship of Christian Athletes Bowl Breakfast, San Diego, CA,
   December 28, 2010.

2. Tim Elmore, *Artificial Maturity: Helping Kids Meet the Challenge of Becoming Authentic Adults*
   (San Francisco: Jossey-Bass, 2012), 71.

Chapter Three

1. Jonah Lehrer, "Don't! The Secret of Self-Control," *The New Yorker,* May 18, 2009, http://www
   .newyorker.com/reporting/2009/05/18/090518fa_fact_lehrer.

2. John Maxwell, *Leadership 101: What Every Leader Needs to Know* (Nashville, TN: Thomas Nelson, 2002), n.p.

Chapter Four

1. Linda and Richard Eyre, *How to Talk to Your Child About Sex* (New York: Macmillan, 1998), 28.
2. Jim Burns, *Teaching Your Children Healthy Sexuality* (Grand Rapids, MI: Bethany House, 2008), 69.
3. Eyre, *How to Talk to Your Child About Sex,* 27.
4. Laurie Langford, *The Big Talk* (New York: John Wiley & Sons, Inc., 1998), 38.
5. J. Thomas Fitch, ed., *Questions Kids Ask About Sex: Honest Answers for Every Age* (Grand Rapids, MI: Revell, 2005), 77.
6. Langford, *The Big Talk,* 26.
7. Eyre, *How to Talk to Your Child About Sex,* 27.
8. Laurie Berkenkamp and Steven C. Atkins, *Talking to Your Kids About Sex: Toddlers to Preteens* (Chicago: Nomad Press, 2002), 30.
9. Carolyn Nystrom, *Before I Was Born* (Colorado Springs: NavPress, 1995), n.p.
10. Fitch, *Questions Kids Ask About Sex,* 80.

Chapter Five

1. "Earthquake Facts and Preparedness," County of San Diego, accessed October 26, 2012, http://sdcounty.ca.gov/oes/disaster_preparedness/oes_jl_earthquakes.html.
2. Stan and Brenna Jones, *How and When to Tell Your Kids About Sex* (Colorado Springs, CO: NavPress, 2007), 14.
3. J. Thomas Fitch, ed., *Questions Kids Ask About Sex: Honest Answers for Every Age* (Grand Rapids, MI: Revell, 2005), 80.
4. Jones, *How and When to Tell Your Kids About Sex,* 78.
5. Laurie Berkenkamp and Steven C. Atkins, *Talking to Your Kids About Sex: Toddlers to Preteens* (Chicago: Nomad Press, 2002), 34.
6. Mark Laaser, *Talking to Your Kids About Sex* (Colorado Springs: WaterBrook, 1999), 108.
7. Ibid., 107.
8. Jones, *How and When to Tell Your Kids About Sex,* 93.
9. "The Profile of a Pedophile," April 14, 2008, http://suite101.com/article/the-profile-of-a-pedophile-a50767.
10. Laaser, *Talking to Your Kids About Sex,* 109.
11. Jones, *How and When to Tell Your Kids About Sex,* 94.

Chapter Six

1. William Tracy, "The Restless Sands," *Saudi Aramco World,* May–June 1965, 1–9, http://www.saudiaramcoworld.com/issue/196503/the.restless.sands.htm.
2. Stan and Brenna Jones, *How and When to Tell Your Kids About Sex* (Colorado Springs, CO: NavPress, 2007), 150.
3. Mark Laaser, *Talking to Your Kids About Sex* (Colorado Springs: WaterBrook, 1999).
4. Linda and Richard Eyre, *How to Talk to Your Child About Sex* (New York: Macmillan, 1998), 16, 52.

5. Ibid., 76.

6. Laaser, *Talking to Your Kids About Sex*, 95.

7. Jones, *How and When to Tell Your Kids About Sex*, 123-4.

8. Ibid., 68.

Chapter Seven

1. Jill Savage and Pam Farrel, *Got Teens?* (Eugene, OR: Harvest House Publishers, 2005), 14-17. Quotations in this section are taken from: Claudia Wallis and Kristina Dell, "What Makes Teens Tick," *Time,* September 26, 2008, http://www.time.com/time/magazine /article/0,9171,994126,00.html.

2. Mark Laaser, *Talking to Your Kids About Sex* (Colorado Springs: WaterBrook, 1999), 39.

3. You can find more information on the Modern-Day Princess ministry at www.modern dayprincess.net and www.saveourgirls.org.

4. "Abstinence Education Supported by 76% of Democratic Parents and 87% of Republican Parents," National Abstinence Education Association, October 13, 2012, http://www.abstinence association.org/newsroom/both_parties_agree_on_sra_ed.html.

5. Leigh Jones, "CDC Reports Show Increase in Abstinence," *Religion Today,* December 4, 2011, http://www.religiontoday.com/news/cdc-reports-show-increase-in-abstinence.html.

6. Kirk Johnson, Jennifer Marshall, and Robert Rector. "Teens Who Make Virginity Pledges Have Substantially Improved Life Outcomes," The Heritage Foundation, September 21, 2004, http://www.heritage.org/research/reports/2004/09/teens-who-make-virginity-pledges-have -substantially-improved-life-outcomes#_ftn1.

7. Josh McDowell and Dick Day, *How to Be a Hero to Your Kids* (Nashville: Thomas Nelson, 1993), 28.

Chapter Eight

1. Anecdote related on "Kids Say the Funniest Things," accessed October 30, 2012, http://kidtips .com/kids.php.

2. Stan and Brenna Jones, *How and When to Tell Your Kids About Sex* (Colorado Springs, CO: NavPress, 2007), 155-56.

3. Nancy Ammon Jianakoplos and Alexandra Bernasek, "Are Women More Risk Averse?" *Economic Inquiry* 36, no. 4 (October 1998): 620-30, doi: 10.1111/j.1465-7295.1998.tb01740.x.

4. Daniel Canary, Tara Emmers-Sommer, and Sandra Faulkner, *Sex and Gender Differences in Personal Relationships* (New York: Guilford Press, 1997), 89-90.

5. "U.S. Adults Estimate That 25% of Americans Are Gay or Lesbian," Gallup Politics, May 27, 2011, http://www.gallup.com/poll/147824/Adults-Estimate-Americans-Gay-Lesbian.aspx.

6. "Gallup Study: 3.4 Percent of US Adults Are LGBT," The Williams Institute, October 18, 2012, http://williamsinstitute.law.ucla.edu/press/gallup-study-3-4-percent-of-us-adults-are-lgbt/.

7. "Marriage Talking Points," National Organization for Marriage, accessed October 30, 2012, http://www.nationformarriage.org/site/c.omL2KeN0LzH/b.4475595/k.566A/Marriage _Talking_Points.htm.

8. "This Is About Our Children," National Organization for Marriage, October 27, 2012, http:// www.nomblog.com/29859/.

Chapter Nine

1. Julie Hiramine, *Guardians of Purity* (Lake Mary, FL: Charisma House, 2012), 25-37.

2. Kris Vallotton, *Moral Revolution: The Naked Truth About Sexual Purity* (Ventura, CA: Regal Publishers, 2012).

3. Maureen Salamon, "Teen Pregnancy Needs to Be De-Glamorized, Experts Say," Children's Health on NBC News, October 20, 2010, http://www.msnbc.msn.com/id/39759635/ns/health-kids_and_parenting/.

4. "Teen Pregnancy Prevention: Making a Difference for At-Risk Populations," National Conference of State Legislatures, accessed October 31, 2012, http://www.ncsl.org/documents/health/teenpregnancy09.pdf.

5. "Parents' Influence on Adolescents' Sexual Behavior," The Heritage Foundation, accessed October 31, 2012, http://www.familyfacts.org/briefs/42/parents-influence-on-adolescents-sexual-behavior.

6. Ibid.

7. "Abortion," Planned Parenthood, accessed October 31, 2012, http://www.plannedparenthood.org/health-topics/abortion-4260.asp.

8. Lawrence B. Finer et al., "Reasons U.S. Women Have Abortions: Quantitative and Qualitative Perspectives," *Perspectives on Sexual and Reproductive Health* 37, no. 3 (2007): 110-18, doi: 10.1111/j.1931-2393.2005.tb00045.x.

9. Rebecca Downs, "A Pro-Life View During Sexual Assault Awareness Month," Life News, April 24, 2012, http://www.lifenews.com/2012/04/24/a-pro-life-view-during-sexual-assault-awareness-month/.

10. Amy Sobie, "What About Abortion in Cases of Rape and Incest? Women and Sexual Assault," Life News, April 5, 2010, http://www.lifenews.com/2010/04/05/nat-6223/.

11. Jasper Williams, Jr., testimony before the U.S. Senate Judiciary Subcommittee on the Constitution Hearings on Constitutional Amendments Relating to Abortion, October 19, 1981, http://www.nrlc.org/abortion/pba/HowOftenAbortionNecessarySaveMother.pdf.

12. Don Sloan and Paula Hartz, Choice: *A Doctor's Experience with the Abortion Dilemma* (New York: International Publishers, 2002), 46.

13. "Are There Rare Cases When an Abortion Is Justified?" Association of Prolife Physicians, accessed October 31, 2012, http://www.prolifephysicians.org/rarecases.htm.

14. Finer, "Reasons U.S. Women Have Abortions," 117.

15. Ibid., 115.

16. Sobie, "What About Abortion in Cases of Rape and Incest?"

Chapter Ten

1. Sharon Jayson, "Sooner vs. Later: Is There an Ideal Age for First Marriage?" *USA Today,* November 9, 2008, http://usatoday30.usatoday.com/news/health/2008-11-09-delayed-marriage_N.htm.

2. Glenn Stanton, "What Is the Best Age to Marry?" Focus on the Family, February 2011, http://www.focusonthefamily.com/about_us/focus-findings/marriage/what-is-the-best-age-to-marry.aspx.

3. Jayson, "Sooner vs. Later."

4. Anne Reiner, "Want to Harm Your Future Marriage? Try Cohabitation," Crosswalk, October 10, 2012, http://www.crosswalk.com/family/marriage/engagement-newlyweds/want-to-harm-your-future-marriage-try-cohabitation.html.

5. Jayson, "Sooner vs. Later."

6. Mark Gungor, quoted in "Knot Now, Americans Say," *The Washington Times,* September 6, 2006, http://www.washingtontimes.com/news/2006/sep/6/20060906-113145-4882r/.

7. Jim Burns, *Teaching Your Children Healthy Sexuality* (Grand Rapids, MI: Bethany House, 2008), 25.

8. Reiner, "Want to Harm Your Future Marriage?"

9. Marian Wallace and Vanessa Warner, "Abstinence: Why Sex Is Worth the Wait," Concerned Women for America, September 5, 2002, http://famguardian.org/Subjects/SexualImmorality/Fornication/Abstinence.htm.

  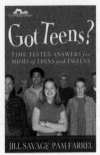 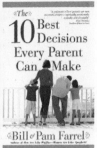

- What does God say about relationships?
- When am I responsible enough to date?
- What role do parents play in all this?
- How can I avoid toxic relationships or unhealthy people?
- How far should I go physically?
- As things get more serious, how do I move the relationship forward in a healthy way?
- How do I know if a relationship needs to end?
- How can I avoid temptation, dangerous situations, or foolish decisions in relationships?
- How do I know I've found "the one"?

Find the answers to these and many more questions in Bill and Pam's other books! And be sure to visit them at www.love-wise.com to find other tools to help launch your teen or young adult, including "Dates to Decide," "The Teen Relationship Contract," and "The Freshman Foundation Dinner and Dialogue Discussions."

For more resources to enhance your relationships and build marriages, or to connect with Bill and Pam Farrel for a speaking engagement, contact

Love-Wise
3755 Avocado Boulevard, #414
La Mesa, CA 91941
800-810-4449
info@Love-Wise.com
www.Love-Wise.com